CH00779837

a p

RHYME

Imagination for a new generation

2006 Poetry Competition for 7-11 year-olds

YoungWriters

Future Voices
Edited by Lynsey Hawkins

 Young**Writers**

First published in Great Britain in 2007 by:
Young Writers
Remus House
Coltsfoot Drive
Peterborough
PE2 9JX
Telephone: 01733 890066
Website: www.youngwriters.co.uk

All Rights Reserved

© Copyright Contributors 2007

SB ISBN 978-1 84602 881 6

Foreword

Young Writers was established in 1991 and has been passionately devoted to the promotion of reading and writing in children and young adults ever since. The quest continues today. Young Writers remains as committed to the nurturing of poetic and literary talent as ever.

This year's Young Writers competition has proven as vibrant and dynamic as ever and we are delighted to present a showcase of the best poetry from across the UK and in some cases overseas. Each poem has been selected from a wealth of *A Pocketful Of Rhyme* entries before ultimately being published in this, our fourteenth primary school poetry series.

Once again, we have been supremely impressed by the overall quality of the entries we have received. The imagination, energy and creativity which has gone into each young writer's entry made choosing the poems a challenging and often difficult but ultimately hugely rewarding task - the general high standard of the work submitted ensured this opportunity to bring their poetry to a larger appreciative audience.

We sincerely hope you are pleased with this final collection and that you will enjoy *A Pocketful Of Rhyme Future Voices* for many years to come.

Contents

Savannah Dallas (10)	20
Jordan Crownshaw (10)	20
Katie McGuiness (10)	21
Lindi Dlamani (10)	21

Dawley CE Primary School, Telford

Emily Walker (11)	22
Shane Butcher (10)	22
Sam Bell (9)	23
Holly Newnes (9)	23
Joseph Mottershaw (10)	24
Daniel Link (9)	24
Amy Maxwell (9)	25
Ben Pritchard (9)	25

Great Heath Primary School, Mildenhall

Luke Edgeworth (8)	26
Ben Cole (8)	26
Chloe Human (8)	27
Craig Langdon (8)	27
Chloe Gilbert (8)	28
Vienna Watts (8)	28
Liam Twyman (8)	29
Ellis Briggs (8)	29
Ellanee Johnson (8)	30
Danny Ryan (8)	30
Michael Brown (7)	31
Zoe Fuller (9)	31
Miles Stiddard (9)	32

Nightingale First School, Norwich

Finlay Payne (7)	32
Finley Taylor (7)	32
Leila Touhami (7)	33
William Savage (7)	33
Hollie Shepherd (7)	34
Joshua Woodward (7)	34
Elizabeth Penwill (7)	35
Sophie Tooke (7)	35
Jordan Mather (7)	36
Misha Coman (7)	36

Alexander Jarvis (7)   37
Katie Ward (7)   37
Fern Attoe (7)   38
Erin Guyton (7)   38
Ryan Watling (7)   39
Ryan George (7)   39
Rachel Jackson (7)   40
Drew Dobson (7)   40
Heidi Burgess (7)   41
Jack Bartram (7)   41
Megan Ward (8)   42
Kayla Woods (7)   42
Sabina Illing (7)   43
Joshua Wymer (7)   43
Jasmine Thompson (7)   44
India Fincham (7)   44

Oak Green School, Aylesbury

Matthew Ireland (7)   45
George Guy (9)   45
Lauren Howard (9)   46
Lucy Cheriman (7)   46
Shauntay Francis (7)   47
Amy Williams (8)   47
Amy Turnbull (8)   48
Alexander Newman (7)   48
Nazmin Akhtar (8)   48
Leighonnie Gardener-Ward (8)   49
Lauren Perry (8)   49
Tahir Taybah (8)   49
Aishah Kamran (7)   50
Erin McCarthy (7)   50
Chantelle McNally (7)   50
Fathema Begum (9)   51
Fazeela Anwar (8)   51
Emily-Rose Baughan (8)   52
Stuart Humphries (8)   52
Shannon Byrne (8)   52
Sadia Fazal (9)   53
Islam Udeen (9)   53
Jack White (8)   54

Humza Abdul Rehman (8)   54
Tessa Avis (8)   55
Jade Andre (8)   55
Afzaal Hussain (8)   55
Amber Colley (8)   56
Amreen Ali (8)   57
Callum Fallows (8)   57

Our Lady & St Oswald's Catholic Primary School, Oswestry
Hannah Greig (8)   57
Michael Hare (7)   58
Niamh Maguire (8)   58
Amelia Gregory (8)   59
Hannah Beaman (8)   59
Alastair Edwards (8)   60
Georgia Dale (8)   60
Emma Jones (7)   61

Randlay Primary School, Telford
Callum Rose (10)   61
Laura Pallett (11)   62

Rushbury CE Primary School, Church Stretton
Adam Young (10)   63
Roisin Goode & Sarah Griffiths (9)   63
Maia Hawthorne (9)   63
Owen Hotchkiss (9)   64
Samuel Pratt (9)   64
James Groves (11)   65
Joe Jones (10)   65
Kate Woodcock (10)   66
Charlie Lippitt (10)   66
Ellie Bytheway (10)   67
Georgina Morris (10)   67
Tom James Carter (9)   68
Chrissie Schlank & Amy Caine   68
Rosalyn Price & Rachel Foster (9)   69
Amy Caine (10)   69
Stephen James Bertie Barnfield (9)   70
William J Lea (10)   70

St Ippolyts CE Primary School, Hitchin

St Patrick's Primary School, Downpatrick

Tara McCrissican (8)	84
Orla Byrne (9)	85
Alexander McCormick (8)	85
Rachel Heathwood (8)	85
Rian Tempany (8)	86
Charlie Power (8)	86
Seamus Walsh (8)	86
Declan Trainor (8)	87
Olivia McCrissican (8)	87

St Patrick's RC Primary School, Telford

Andrew Haynes (11)	87
Liam Flynn (10)	88
Eilish Ryan (11)	89
Lauren Gould (10)	90
Luke Jekiel (10)	90
Sam Doody (10)	91
Tabitha Heeley (11)	91
Sarah Pearson (10)	92
Lauren Morgan (11)	93
Georgia Cruise (10)	94
Kieran Jones (10)	95
Joseph Broad (10)	96
Adassa Palmer (10)	96

Stoke on Tern Primary School, Market Drayton

Katy Aylward (9)	97
Charis Virgo (9)	97
Benjamin Viggars (7)	98
Kallum Brian (8)	99
Jessica Thomson (7)	100
Molly Marfleet (7)	101
Oliver Emmerson (7)	102
Erin Drakard (7)	103
Rowena Tustin (7)	104
James Whittaker (7)	105
Kim Orme (7)	106
Ben Preece (7)	107
Serena Talbot (7)	108
Robert Humphris (9)	108
Isabel Randall (7)	109

The Poems

The Art Of War

I'm mourning, the crows fly above,
I've lost my life,
Of which I did love,
The fall of the knife . . .

Which ended my life . . .

Pain from the left,
Pain from the right,
This was a theft,
Of which I had no sight . . .

I was hidden from the light . . .

I watched as my friends did fall,
I stood watching, with appal,
Men lay helpless on the ground,
I felt an emotion, it was astound . . .

What horror, the men took their last sound . . .

I felt my heart miss a beat,
It was in the air, I smelt defeat.
Then it came, I hit the ground,
This bothered me, where was the sound . . . ?

A sword hit me, blood flooded the ground . . .

We had lost,
My heart would not defrost.
I lay tattered on the floor,
Then the enemy bellowed a roar . . .

This is the art of war.

Jack Elliott Orr (10)

My First Of Five

An apple is a good start.
Rosy-red apple like a small ball.
Lemons are good after, small and juicy.
Broccoli is very good in a dinner.
Green like a small tree.
Red grapes are good too,
Small, squidgy and fresh.
Coconuts are good too,
Brown like a football, fresh, minty and solid.

James Cantrill (7)

Beautiful

I look into the mirror and who do I see?
I see my mother staring back at me.
She tells me I'm beautiful,
Oh how I miss her now she's gone.

Hannah Swan (10)

My Sister

Her scream is like a foghorn
That is heard in the USA,
It would knock down a building,
It would make Mount Everest have an avalanche
That would crush ten people.

Oliver Coleyshaw (9)

Teacher

T eachers are fantastic
E very child works hard to get an . . .
A* because it is the highest mark
C omfort and help is what teachers do.
H ow hard can it be to be a teacher?
E asy I think, but sometimes not because . . .
R ows and noise makes you have a headache.

Anisa Nazir (9)

Charlie

Charlie
Cheerful, funny.
Tig, football, hide-and-seek.
He is always funny.
Charles.

James Donald (7)

Sadness

Sadness is blue like a fast falling teardrop
Sadness tastes like dark blood as red as a rose
Sadness sounds like spine-tingling screeching screams
Sadness smells like rotten, old mouldy cheese
Sadness looks like the darkness of midnight
Sadness feels like a heart-crushing pain
Sadness reminds me of a weeping, lonely child with nowhere to go.

Lucy Gerrard (10)

The House, The First Time

'What is that plank of wood, Mother,
That holds metal and cheese,
It tempts me with its orangey look,
Oh, Mother, can I take a bite please?'

'It is a mousetrap, my dear son,
And *no*, you may not take a bite!
It is a weapon of mousey destruction
Against all of micekind.'

'What is that lump of peach colour,
That moves back and forth;
It jumps up and down,
And grates all that lovely cheese?'

'That is a foot of a man, dear son,
It drops all of the crumbs for our tea,
That is where the mousetraps come from, dear,
So never, never go near!'

'What is that grey thing, Mother,
That creeps, pads and claws,
Makes a funny noise like a purr,
And scratches up the walls?'

'It is a cat, my dear son,
It is a fierce, fiery animal.
It streaks along the ground in a hurry,
It could catch you in a flurry.'

'What is that thing that follows me,
As black as night after day;
It copies my every movement,
And takes a dive for my food?'

'That is your shadow, my dear son,
Closer to you than me or your brother,
Every mouse has one, don't be ashamed,
For it is you yourself you see!'

Sophie Hammond (10)
Ashford Carbonell CE Primary School, Ludlow

My Poem About A Bully Named Joe

Bully Joe is a kid I know
Who is as mean as a grizzly bear.
He is tall and he is strong.
We just don't get along.
There is not one thing in common we share.

When a kid's pants fall off
You know Joe took out the strings.
Joe likes to torture little ones
That's how he gets his grins.

When there's gum in someone's hair,
You know it's Joe who blew the bubble.
When the teacher shouts, 'Whoooooo!'
You know Bully Joe's in big trouble.

When something does not agree with Joe
He argues until he wins.
He likes to fight.
He also likes to kick people in their shins.

He calls us nasty names
To kids who do their own thing.
If he saw an injured kid,
He would laugh until he was sick.

Bully Joe
Is a kid I know
Who does not have one single friend
And never will he do so . . .

Umar Khan (10)
Bramingham Primary School, Luton

The Frog And The Toad

There was an old fogey across the road,
Who owned a frog and a toad,
He always fed them every day,
Before they went out to play.

They hopped around the garden,
Both night and day,
Until their owner said,
'I want to give you away.'

Both frog and toad were devastated,
Their hearts and souls became deflated,
They never found better owners,
I guess you could call them Larry Loners.

They found a new home,
Next to a garden gnome,
With flower beds,
To lay their heads.

It was ever so peaceful,
Where they now lived,
It seemed to be a wonderful gift.

Lauren Connelly (10)
Bramingham Primary School, Luton

Water

Without water our country would be a mess
Everybody would be in agony and stress
If we did not have water we would not survive
So be thankful to God He keeps you alive.

Everybody has a right to drink water
It is not fair that some countries are in a mess
So let's all join hands and help
The countries who have less.

Shane Packham (9)
Bramingham Primary School, Luton

Roses

Roses come in lots of colours,
Red, blue, yellow or pink,
Which colour is best?
What do you think?

Roses come in lots of colours,
Shapes and sizes too,
They brighten up any place,
With smells for me and you.

Roses are more than flowers,
You send them to show your love,
Roses grow under the burning sun,
And the blue sky above.

Jade Stephens (10)
Bramingham Primary School, Luton

My World

In my world . . .
The grass would be blue
And the sky would be green.
The sun would be red
And give a purple sheen.
In my world . . .
People would walk on their hands
And stand up when they are asleep
They'd wear shoes on their hands
And gloves on their feet.
This is my world . . .
It's a bit upside down
Don't you think?

Rebecca Cooper (10)
Bramingham Primary School, Luton

The Explosion At Buncefield

It was a cold December morning when the explosion woke me.
I nearly fell out of bed. Chills went down my spine. *Bang!*
At first I thought it was thunder
No, it was something much worse.

Everybody woke in the house as more bangs were heard.
The dog was barking, the phone was ringing!
Was it a firework? Was it thunder?
No, it had to be something much worse.

I thought it was nothing, it turned out to be a surprise.
The explosion at Buncefield could have killed a lot.
It turned out to be a lucky event since no one died.
God bless the people at work.
Was it a firework? Was it some thunder?
No, it turned out to be something much worse.

Aiden Kelly (10)
Bramingham Primary School, Luton

Grandma

My granny was special in many ways.
She liked to make you laugh.
She would tell me, 'It's time to take your bath.'

Her smile always brightened up your day.
Her voice was very loud and clear.

Her cooking was the best.
Especially her cakes, she made all kinds,
Fairy cakes and birthday cakes
But don't forget her West Indian bakes.

I will never forget my granny.

Kofi Woodley (9)
Bramingham Primary School, Luton

Strong

The walk to school is lonely
She's suddenly pushed to the ground
They say they're just messing around
They call her a freak
They say she's just weak
They're wrong
She's strong.

By playtime her trousers are torn
She has scratches down her face
Yet she carries on
She knows the day will be long
She doesn't care
She'll still stand strong.

At the end of the day
She wants to hide
As she knows the bullies will try to take her pride
They're wrong
She'll stay strong.

Ellie Still   (10)
Bramingham Primary School, Luton

A Maths Problem

There is one thing I don't agree,
In mathematics you see,
Is why degrees
Means the same, I'm sure
In angles and in temperature?

It has aroused a great suspicion
Amongst the children in tuition
Why can't we measure angles in tinks or yolks?
To stop the teachers cracking stupid jokes!

Rebecca Preston   (11)
Bramingham Primary School, Luton

My Brother's Toys

My brother's toys are everywhere,
Trains under the sofa
And books sat on chairs.

He leaves them in my bedroom,
He leaves them on the floor,
When I go to pick them up,
He's busy dropping more!

My brother's toys are everywhere,
Teddies in the toy box
And balls on the stairs.

I find them in the bath,
I find them in the sink,
He's dropped one down the toilet,
Into the bin, I think!

My brother's toys are everywhere,
Cars on the carpet
And bricks in a square.

My brother's toys are *everywhere!*

Anya Lotay (10)
Bramingham Primary School, Luton

Dolphins

Shiny grey in the deep blue sea.
Their beautiful eyes say come play with me.
Splishing and splashing as they dive through the waves.
Somersaults in the evening haze.

Dolphins are wonderful, intelligent and bright.
I wish I could see one every night.
What would the world be without these creatures?
Please don't harm them and their lovely features.

Aliyah Ahmed (10)
Bramingham Primary School, Luton

In My Cupboard . . .

It's dark and scary,
I'm sure I saw something hairy.
He was big and pink,
and he really did stink.

He's been there for years,
so he's grown massive ears.
He has really long nails,
and I think he eats snails.

He picks his nose
and nibbles his toes.
He's really, really dumb,
I've seen him sucking his thumb.

His teeth are all wonky,
he sounds like a donkey.
He's too fat and slow,
He's just got to go.

Samuel Coombes (11)
Bramingham Primary School, Luton

Limericks

There once was a lady from Hong Kong
Who like to play her song
So she went to the park
Sang with Mark
And then she went to see King Kong.

There once was a lady from Beijing
Who really liked to sing
So she went to the 'X Factor'
Then drove a tractor
And then she sang with the king.

Chloe Northwood (11)
Bramingham Primary School, Luton

Sleepover

Will they be early?
Will they be late?
My sleepover friends
Are all my best mates.

The time is now seven,
Why aren't they here?
The doorbell soon rings,
I give a big cheer!

We run up the stairs,
As fast as can be,
We're all so excited,
My friends and me.

A midnight feast,
We cannot wait,
But Mum soon shouts,
'It's getting late!'

We eat and drink
Until it's all gone,
Then have a dance
And one or two songs.

Eventually we fall asleep,
The time is very late.
I'm just so glad my sleepover,
Was with all my best mates!

Nicola Heggie (10)
Bramingham Primary School, Luton

Winter Is . . .

Winter is icy and cold
it is snowy and white.
People wearing hats and gloves
but the best thing about
winter is Christmas!

Lydia Wallace (10)
Bramingham Primary School, Luton

Fun In The Sun

I went to Spain
On an aeroplane
It rained and rained
Oh what a shame.

We played a game
And I hurt my brain
So we took the train
To sort the pain.

I needed a pee
So I went to the sea
I crouched on my knees
And I saw a lot of seaweed.

We went to the park
When it was dark
We had a laugh
I played with a giraffe.

There was no sun
We had no fun
I sat on my bum
And nothing was done.

So this rhyme ends
Driving you round the bend
It's what we intend
But it's the end.

Stefan Man (10)
Bramingham Primary School, Luton

Boy From Spain

There once was a boy from Spain
Who went on a train
He felt great
He met his mate
And they went down Park Lane.

Demi Page (11)
Bramingham Primary School, Luton

Five Little Elves

Five little elves playing by the shore
One sailed away and then there were four.

Four little elves climbed up a tree
One of them fell down and then there were three.

Three little elves found a pot of glue
One got stuck in then there were two.

Two little elves found a currant bun
One ran away with it then there was one.

One little elf cried all afternoon
So they put him in an aeroplane and sent him to the moon.

Rhys Felix (9)
Bramingham Primary School, Luton

Summer Season

Summer season in the sun,
Children having fantastic fun.
While teachers pout,
All the children shout,
'Let's have great fun!'

Teachers drinking cups of tea,
They're all the same, like you and me.
Playtime's over,
Teachers get off the sofa,
Come back to class and teach me.

Demi Owens (10)
Bramingham Primary School, Luton

Soozie

My aunt's dog Soozie is a right little terror
But buying her was not an error.

She likes to run around and bark
But sleeps like a puppy when it gets dark.

She is black and gorgeous and I love her so
One day I hope she'll win the dog show.

She pants and sniffs and nibbles at my ears
And when I am sad she licks away my tears.

I hope she will always be my friend
But one day I know it will come to an end.

Reece Cray (11)
Bramingham Primary School, Luton

Football

Football is the game I love to play
Saturdays and Sundays I'm always on the pitch
No matter what the weather is I will be out all day
Hopefully this will all pay off and one day I will be rich.

At last we've kicked off, here we go
At last I hear the whistle blow
I am heading towards the goal
When I shoot and it hits the pole
On we go, the ball is kicked down
Oh yes, I just scored, what a goal!

Sam Flannery (10)
Bramingham Primary School, Luton

Holiday

I'm going on holiday
To hot sunny Spain,
I'm not going by car,
I'm going on a plane.

We're going to take off,
The plane starts to move,
I feel the excitement,
All the way through.

I'm starving to death,
And as thirsty as can be,
I need to eat soon,
And so does my family.

I can't wait any longer,
We're now nearly there,
I'm airsick and sticky,
But I don't really care.

We're finally there,
I'm jet-lagged and hot,
I'm now in Madrid,
And I like it a lot.

Jasraj Singh Jandu (10)
Bramingham Primary School, Luton

The Best Player

I am a football fan,
I play it whenever I can.
My favourite player is Ronaldinho,
He is a midfield maestro,
He is the best in the world,
When they made him they broke the mould.
Barcelona is my favourite team,
To play for them would be my dream.

Glenn Jarvis (10)
Bramingham Primary School, Luton

My Rabbit Marmite

Marmite is my rabbit,
He hops about all day,
He wanders in the garden,
But never runs away.

He loves it when it's meal time,
It's his favourite part of the day,
Carrots, lettuce and rabbit food,
Soon get put away.

Marmite's cage is made of wood,
We fill it up with straw
So he is nice and cosy,
When he goes in the door.

Marmite has loppy ears,
That's his breed you know,
He eats my mum's flowers,
What a little so and so!

Rebecca Heggie (10)
Bramingham Primary School, Luton

I Play

I play on my computer on Monday,
I play football for my school on Tuesday,
I play with my friends on Wednesday,
I play with my PlayStation on Thursday,
I play my music on Friday,
I play for a football team on Saturday,
I wake up late on Sunday,
Because that's my *fun day!*

Matthew Kirby-Daniels (11)
Bramingham Primary School, Luton

The Menu

All kinds of lovely food,
Really puts *me* in the mood,
To cook a really exotic thing,
Makes my tastebuds ting-a-ling.

The look of fish may not be nice,
Keeping cool, covered in ice,
But cook it with some lemon and herb,
Turns it into something superb.

A roasted lamb for a Sunday lunch,
It's so tender, there's no need to munch,
It melts in your mouth, the flavour is great,
The dinner's so nice, I've cleared my plate.

All types of rainbow-coloured veg,
On the plate, sitting round the edge,
Lots of veg keeps you healthy and fit,
Make sure you eat every last little bit.

Puddings are such a treat,
They are so lovely, and taste so sweet,
Too many of them is not so great,
It will easily make you put on weight.

Be a taste tester and try new food,
It will really put *you* in the mood,
Just like me, give everything a try,
It's time for my dinner, so I'll say, 'Goodbye.'

Thomas Yeatman (10)
Bramingham Primary School, Luton

My Rhyming Alphabet

A nts crawling on the grass,
B ats flying over to France.
C rows pecking anywhere near,
D eers having a lot more cheer.
E lephants standing really tall,
F oxes crouching very small.
G erbils nibbling many places,
H ammerkop flying in large spaces.
I nsects digging same as moles,
J aguars leaping over holes.
K angaroos jumping super high,
L adybirds flapping their wings to fly.
M onkeys grabbing onto trees,
N ewts are so easily pleased.
O ctopus has cold blood,
P igs roll in dirty mud.
Q uails are a type of bird,
R hinos can always be heard.
S nakes slither to catch their prey,
T urtles are always awake in the day.
U mbrella fish swimming in the sea,
V ultures flying over me.
W hales splashing everywhere,
X antus hummingbirds eating pears.
Y aks sliding down snowy hills,
Z ebras never eat animals with gills.

Brandon Beaumont (10)
Bramingham Primary School, Luton

Feelings

Happiness is calm,
Happiness is great,
Happiness is sometimes the number 8.

Sadness is rough,
Sadness is bad,
Sadness is something I've already had.

Anger is hurtful,
Anger is scary,
Anger is nothing, nothing like a fairy.

Love is big,
Love is small,
Love is also, also very tall.

Savannah Dallas (10)
Bramingham Primary School, Luton

Mnemonic

G oldilocks ate the bears' porridge,
O h no, what a pity,
L ook, she's broken a chair,
D ozing in bed,
 I n came the bears,
L ook who's that there?
O ut, out of here,
C atch her, catch her,
K ick her out of here,
S tick her in gaol.

Jordan Crownshaw (10)
Bramingham Primary School, Luton

Rainbow

Red is the colour of a rose
like the colour of my lips.
Blue is the colour of a violet
budding in the spring.
Green is the colour of grass
where I lie and dream.
Yellow is the colour of the daffodil
it is as tall as a tower.
Purple is the colour of a pansy
blowing in the wind.
Orange is the colour of the sun
where I lie and sunbathe.

Katie McGuiness (10)
Bramingham Primary School, Luton

View From My Window

Fab February
Leaves as white as snow,
The crystal rose falls to the white earth.
High in the sky
A swallow flies around
The beautiful sky, across waves of silvery clouds.

Trees bend, snow falls,
The drops knock at the window
And my warm heart lets it in.

Lindi Dlamani (10)
Bramingham Primary School, Luton

The Iron Man

The howling sound across the hill,
The sound of metal pins,
He eats the metal, he kills the metal,
Kill, kill, kill!
The iron man is coming.

With his shining armour of metal,
Eating metal wire, chewing, chewing,
Stealing this, stealing that,
Anything with metal,
The iron man is back.

The trap is set
For someone very big
Trick, trick, trick
The iron man is in.

We got him in the trap,
We got him, we got him,
We got him in the trap,
Is it the end for the iron man?

Emily Walker (11)
Dawley CE Primary School, Telford

The Iron Man

His arms are made of steel,
If he could he would eat
A giant metal barbed wire reel.
The iron man is coming,
The rusty van is humming.
His iron hair comes very rare,
His shoulder is like
A great metal boulder.

Shane Butcher (10)
Dawley CE Primary School, Telford

Waterfall

The water speedily coming down,
Splish, splash, splosh,
The feeling is wonderful
When standing on the ground.
The rocky mountain surrounding the water,
On the top it's nervous when you're looking down,
It's really great when it's a secret place,
Splish, splash, splosh.

The trees stand tall,
With a whispering call,
Just jump in the water, they say,
At the bottom of the waterfall, it's glistening and sparkling
With a Christmas feeling.
Joyful and ecstatic,
Your toes twinkle,
Your body feels warm.

Sam Bell (9)
Dawley CE Primary School, Telford

St Lucia

The cold rushing waterfall
and the soft slimy but wet green moss.

The sparkling waterfall, like a thousand lights
on a Christmas tree.

The bold thundering waterfall,
with mist so smooth, it's like you're rubbing
your face on the smooth soft sand.

The rich smell by the waterfall,
of fish as fresh as the cold air.

The newly grown grass by the waterfall,
lie on it when the sun blares down.

Holly Newnes (9)
Dawley CE Primary School, Telford

Captain Bloody Sword

The night was full of staring eyes,
Cyclops stared down with his giant eye,
The darkness was darker than the darkest dark,
Small swishing like the cloak of a thief,
Swish, swish, swish

Shadows passed and nothing moved,
A glint in the darkness,
Red shone bright from the trees,
The trees creaked and fell,
One by one, one by one.

A ghostly figure on the shore,
An eye ablaze, the other a pool of black,
Dressed in rags,
Another glint in the dark,
Menacing face, bloodthirsty face, evil face.

Joseph Mottershaw (10)
Dawley CE Primary School, Telford

The Waterfall

Water going crazily
Crashing down to the bottom
Thundering down, down, down
To the bottom
Thump, thump, thump
As the water bashes to the bottom.
The waterfall powerfully
Thrashing to the bottom.

Daniel Link (9)
Dawley CE Primary School, Telford

The Pirate

He sails through seas,
For months and days,
His crew doing jobs on the deck.

Sometimes it's rough,
Sometimes it's calm,
Steering an old wooden wreck.

His evil eyes stare out
At the sea,
Giving a horrible fright.

He'll travel to the north,
With weather so wet,
His teeth as black as soot.

Amy Maxwell (9)
Dawley CE Primary School, Telford

The Waterfall

The waterfall is frothing down,
The waterfall is bashing and crashing,
All over the place,
But doesn't leave a trace.
The waterfall is booming, zooming down
At the top it's like a crown.

The rock pools on the bottom are bold,
The rock pools are sharp,
The rock pools are a death-trap.

Ben Pritchard (9)
Dawley CE Primary School, Telford

What Parents Say

It's funny what parents say, like
Brush your teeth,
Make your bed.
Can't you make it instead?
Go outside, it's a hot day.
Get in the bath,
Brush your hair,
Go to bed now!
Are you listening?
Wash your hair.
What time do you call this?
Why aren't you in bed yet?
Do you think I'm Wonder Woman?
Put the bin out!

No!
I ain't got no answers!

Luke Edgeworth (8)
Great Heath Primary School, Mildenhall

What Parents Say

It's funny the things that parents say like
Take the bin out!
Clean your room!
Be patient.
What time is it?
Why aren't you dressed?

You're late!
Do I have to repeat myself?
Brush your teeth!
Wash your hair!
Eat your dinner!
Lot's of questions - no answers.

Ben Cole (8)
Great Heath Primary School, Mildenhall

Paradise

If children ruled the world
Bedtimes would be late.
Parents wouldn't do cleaning
And tell us what to do.
Every day would be great.

Holidays would be every month
Swimming pools would be big.
Weekends would be hot
With a massive sun.

Chocolate would be the size of fields
With lollipops,
Growing on trees,
Tree trunks would be jellytots
Growing everywhere.

Bullies would be gone forever
Snow in July, April, May, June
More pets at home,
No more locking gates.

So come on children everywhere,
Right across the land
If only for a day
Let's make sure we get out the way.

Chloe Human (8)
Great Heath Primary School, Mildenhall

What Parents Say

Do you think I'm speaking French?
Do you think I'm Wonder Woman?
Are you a monkey or something?
What will you think of next?
Stop monkeying around!
Do you think I'm a monkey?

Craig Langdon (8)
Great Heath Primary School, Mildenhall

My Ideal World

In my ideal world
there would be lots
of treats just for me.

When I am home I would
play with Bratz and at night
I would cuddle my cat.

At the park I would
ride my bike, that is what
I definitely like.

In the town, on the Jubilee Field
you would see a tent
of funny clowns.

Chloe Gilbert (8)
Great Heath Primary School, Mildenhall

I Hate Bedtime!

Mum! Dad! It's only eight!
You always say eight is late.
I need the loo before bed,
No! No! No, to bed!
Lay your head on the pillow.
Boo! Boo to bedtime!
Out go the lights!
Goodnight! Noo!
Boo! Hoo! Waaa!
I'm ill! You haven't got a temperature
Oh, I give up. I'll have to go to bed.

Vienna Watts (8)
Great Heath Primary School, Mildenhall

If Children Ruled The World

If children ruled the world
Bedtime would be banned
And adults would be sent
To bed early, eight o'clock sharp.

Adults would go to school
Wear a funny uniform
And wear a funny dude hat
And have lots of homework.
They would study all day long.

Sweets and chocolate every day
But pocket money is on weekends.

We would have Xboxes, PlayStation 2
Doughnuts galore
Caramel chunks
With mint and candyfloss too.

Liam Twyman (8)
Great Heath Primary School, Mildenhall

Chocolate Doughnut Land

Think!
Think of Chocolate Doughnut Land,
Where you would have widescreen TV,
And everything is free.
Boys would rule chocolate schools,
Everywhere chocolate doughnuts.
Snow every day,
Ferrari Enzos would be free.
Come on children, now let's rule
The world and have some fun.

Ellis Briggs (8)
Great Heath Primary School, Mildenhall

What Parents Say

It's funny the things parents say, like
What are you doing?
Who do you think you are?
Where do you think you're going?
What are you like?
Do you think I'm your slave?
Do you think I was born yesterday?
Do you think I'm Wonder Woman?
Do you think money grows on trees?
What are you thinking?
When will you learn?
What are you going on about?
Mums never stop talking!

Ellanee Johnson (8)
Great Heath Primary School, Mildenhall

In My Ideal World

I would like chocolate bars
to play all day with my cars
and there also would be,
lovely treats for me.

I would like to see the clowns
parading through the towns,
giving away free ice creams.

All the shops would be closed
at midnight and there will be
free sweets for me and
everyone will *leave me be!*

Danny Ryan (8)
Great Heath Primary School, Mildenhall

What Parents Say

It's funny the things parents say, like
what do you look like?
Why aren't you listening?
Why were you late?
When will you stop acting like a child?
Why are you putting pen lids in your mouth?
Are you up yet?
Why are you filthy?
Why are you playing games all day?

Do I have to repeat myself?
What kind of music do you call that?

Where is your football kit?
Where did you put your book bag?
Why aren't you carrying my things?
What do you call this?

Michael Brown (7)
Great Heath Primary School, Mildenhall

My Ideal World

In my ideal world there would be
lots of lovely treats for me.

I would like to play with my dog
and a friendly frog.

All aunties go to bed at eight
and get grounded for a week
so they won't be out so late.

Dads will go to school with uniforms on
drinking a nice cup of tea
all day long.

Zoe Fuller (9)
Great Heath Primary School, Mildenhall

If Monsters Ruled The World

If monsters ruled the world
It would be a scary place,
There would be all sorts of monsters.
There would be choppers and
Stompers followed by crushers
And mushers with blushers
Flashers and crashers.
If monsters ruled the world.

Miles Stiddard (9)
Great Heath Primary School, Mildenhall

The Magic Box

(Inspired by 'Magic Box' by Kit Wright)

I will put in the box, the taste of pizza,
squishy, with pineapple and ham
I will put in the box, the smell of cream cakes,
squishy and creamy.
I will put in the box, the feel of a fluffy puppy
with a wet nose.
I will put in the box, my necklace,
glassy and colourful.

Finlay Payne (7)
Nightingale First School, Norwich

What Is Red?

Red is a plane, smelly and fast
Red is a plane, comfy and noisy
Red is a table, hard
Red is an apple, juicy and delicious
Red is a water bottle, hard and metal
Red is a pencil, straight and still
Red is a cup, plastic and tall
Red is a nice colour.

Finley Taylor (7)
Nightingale First School, Norwich

The Magic Box

(Inspired by 'Magic Box' by Kit Wright)

I will put in the box the taste of lasagne,
delicious and cheesy.
I will put in the box, the smell of my mum's
favourite flowers, sweet and beautiful.
I will put in the box the feel of my kitten's whiskers,
white and thin.
I will put in the box the sound of my
baby doll crying.
I will put in the box the feel of my furry carpet
sweet and clean.
I will put in the box, a picture of my family.
I will put in the box my best friend's beautiful
pattern, clear and bright.
I will put in the box my Top Trumps,
cool and magnificent.

Leila Touhami (7)
Nightingale First School, Norwich

The Magic Box

(Inspired by 'Magic Box' by Kit Wright)

I will put in the box . . .
The smell of Norwich, dusty and exhausted
The smell of people working hard and quiet.

I will put in the box . . .
The sight of the countryside, calm and nice,
The sight of a baby being born, soft and cute.

I will put in the box . . .
The feel of a football, hard and muddy,
The feel of a bag, strong and heavy.

I will put in the box . . .
The taste of spaghetti, yummy and strong,
The taste of strawberries, sweet and juicy.

William Savage (7)
Nightingale First School, Norwich

The Magic Box

(Inspired by 'Magic Box' by Kit Wright)

I will put in the box . . .
The softness of a baby tiger
The smell of chocolate
And the taste of sweet cakes.

I will put in the box . . .
My necklace with stones on that I can feel
My lavender that smells lovely
And my recorder that is loud.

I will put in the box . . .
A good smell of a rose that is delicate
And a cat that is soft and cute
And a family photo that I can see.

I will put in the box . . .
The taste of a chocolate muffin
The sound of a tweeting bird and
The sound of splashing water.

Hollie Shepherd (7)
Nightingale First School, Norwich

The Magic Box

(Inspired by 'Magic Box' by Kit Wright)

I will put in the box, the taste of chocolate cookies
with icing on the top.
I will put in the box, the smell of banana milkshakes,
creamy and smooth.
I will put in the box, the feel of my baby sister
who is lovely and smooth.
I will put in the box, the sound of the television
loud and quiet.
I will put in the box, my computer, quick
and cool.

Joshua Woodward (7)
Nightingale First School, Norwich

The Magic Box

(Inspired by 'Magic Box' by Kit Wright)

I will put in the box . . .
The taste of a spicy and crunchy chorizo pizza.

I will put in the box . . .
The smell of a crunchy red apple.

I will put in the box . . .
My furry and brown toy lion.

I will put in the box . . .
The sound of a cute and cuddly
guinea pig.

I will put in the box . . .
The feel of a smooth and long
piece of wood.

I will put in the box . . .
The sound of a shiny silver whistle.

I will put in the box . . .
The smell of a green ripe pear.

I will put in the box . . .
The taste of cold and squishy ice cream.

Elizabeth Penwill (7)
Nightingale First School, Norwich

What Is Blue?

Blue is the sea, salty and wavy.
The big rocky mountains, high and silky,
The sand soft and tickly, it always makes me giggle,
The clouds are white, moving fast, so the sky is good as past.

What is pink?

Pink is the pigs oinking and annoying,
Pink is the sky when it is late,
Pink is your skin, squidgy and soft.

Sophie Tooke (7)
Nightingale First School, Norwich

The Magic Box

(Inspired by 'Magic Box' by Kit Wright)

I will put in the box . . .
The smell of garlic bread,
The smell of fresh air.

I will put in the box . . .
The sound of a twittering bird on my head
The sound of a worm, wiggling.

I will put in the box . . .
The sight of soft melting chocolate in my hand,
The sight of a magnificent fly.

I will put in the box . . .
The taste of the salty blue sea in my mouth,
The taste of salty chips.

I will put in the box . . .

Jordan Mather (7)
Nightingale First School, Norwich

The Magic Box

(Inspired by 'Magic Box' by Kit Wright)

I will put in the box . . .
The taste of chocolate, crunchy
and brown.

I will put in the box . . .
The smell of a pizza, tasty
and triangular.

I will put in the box . . .
The feel of my teddy bear
with black eyes.

I will put in the box . . .
The sound of a dog
with its big teeth and nose.

Misha Coman (7)
Nightingale First School, Norwich

The Magic Box

(Inspired by 'Magic Box' by Kit Wright)

I will put in the box . . .
The sight of my exciting micro machines,
The sight of the dinosaur park.

I will put in the box . . .
The sound of the beautiful music coming upstairs.
The sound of birds tweeting.

I will put in the box . . .
The smell of the delicious melting chocolate
The smell of Mummy's cooking.

I will put in the box . . .
The taste of melted chocolate.
The taste of a tasty sausage.

I will put in the box . . .
The feel of a furry cat,
The feel of a snugly cushion.

Alexander Jarvis (7)
Nightingale First School, Norwich

The Magic Box

(Inspired by 'Magic Box' by Kit Wright)

I will put in the box, the taste of
Galaxy chocolate, melting in my mouth.

I will put in the box, the smell of
fresh perfume, rosy and red.

I will put in the box, the feel
of a baby lion cub, cuddly and soft.

I will put in the box, the sound of
birds twittering loudly in the trees.

I will put in the box, the feel of
my bunny rabbit, fluffy and bouncy.

Katie Ward (7)
Nightingale First School, Norwich

The Magic Box

(Based on 'Magic Box' by Kit Wright)

I will put in the box . . .
A yellow fluffy duckling swimming on the pond
A pint milkshake twirling slurping in my mouth
A blue tit singing up in a green tree

Some melted chocolate running in my hand
A horse sniffing in my picnic bag and eating an apple
Some kittens chasing a sneaky mouse

Sea crashing to the seashore,
A rose so red, it smells up my nose

My box is made out of . . .
Silver and gold stars and stripes on the lid
With hearts and diamonds and dots on the front.

Fern Attoe (7)
Nightingale First School, Norwich

The Magic Box

(Inspired by 'Magic Box' by Kit Wright)

I will put in the box . . .
Cold fresh ice cream melting in the sun,
Lovely-shaped earrings sparkling in the light,
A lovely cute cat chasing lots of mice.
Rustling windy leaves waving at me.
A beautiful little rose making me feel happy.

I will put in the box . . .
Soft chocolate cookies yummy! Yummy! Yummy!
Beautiful sweet birds singing lovely songs,
My box is made from gold and silver squares
Blue beautiful jewels with yellow stars.

Erin Guyton (7)
Nightingale First School, Norwich

The Magic Box

(Inspired by 'Magic Box' by Kit Wright)

I will put in the box . . .
The sight of a rough boxer running up a really steep hill.
The sight of my friend at the park playing with me on the swings.
The sight of a lovely kitten running away from a mean dog.

I will put in the box . . .
The smell of a lovely, sweet, yummy cake.
The smell of a stinky-pinky muddy pig.
The smell of a sweet, lovely, sticky chocolate bar.

I will put in the box . . .
The sound of a sweet puppy barking at the top of its voice,
The sound of a beautiful cat, fluffy as can be,
The sound of a ball bouncing on the hard ground.

Ryan Watling (7)
Nightingale First School, Norwich

Magic Box

(Inspired by 'Magic Box' by Kit Wright)

I will put in the box . . .
The sight of my biggest best dog in the world,
The sight of a black, hairy spider making a web.

I will put in the box . . .
The sound of wet, salty rain,
The sound of crunchy autumn leaves in the wind.

I will put in the box . . .
The smell of fish and chips, fresh and hot on my plate,
The smell of fresh chicken cooking in the cooker.

I will put in the box . . .
The taste of smooth bacon sizzling in the pan,
The taste of bubbling beans in the pan.

Ryan George (7)
Nightingale First School, Norwich

The Magic Box

(Inspired by 'Magic Box' by Kit Wright)

I will put in the box . . .
The sight of melting chocolate in
the blazing hot sun.
The sight of my best friend having a water fight
with me.
The sight of lots of robins flying
in the bright sky.

I will put in the box . . .
The sound of my big brother screaming
like a girl.
The sound of lots of birds in the
blue sky.
The sound of laughing children having
lots of fun.

I will put in the box . . .
The smell of runny syrup running
on my toast,
The smell of chocolate ice cream
being made.
The smell of popcorn being eaten.

I will put in the box . . .
The feel of a cute furry kitten.

Rachel Jackson (7)
Nightingale First School, Norwich

The Magic Box

(Based on 'Magic Box' by Kit Wright)

I will put in the box . . .
The beautiful sunset in the sky,
The sweet taste of a salt and vinegar crisp from a shop.

My box is made of . . .
Strips of gold and diamond rings.

Drew Dobson (7)
Nightingale First School, Norwich

Magic Box
(Inspired by 'Magic Box' by Kit Wright)

I will put in the box . . .
The sight of leaves falling off the trees,
The sight of my best friends at school,
The sight of playing with my friend in my bedroom.

I will put in the box . . .
The sound of the wind pushing the leaves off the trees,
The sound of the waves crashing on the seashore,
The sound of pencils drawing on paper.

I will put in the box . . .
The feel of my dog, soft, fluffy and cuddly,
The feel of my rabbit, soft and fluffy,
The feel of my friend's skin,

I will put in the box . . .
The taste of popcorn in the cinema,
The taste of strawberries with sugar,
The taste of bacon sizzling in the pan.

Heidi Burgess (7)
Nightingale First School, Norwich

The Magic Box
(Based on 'Magic Box' by Kit Wright)

I will put in the box . . .

Lovely hot chips,
The smell of roast chicken in the oven,
The sound of the train,
The sound of my dad's car racing,
The soft touch of my cuddly dog.

My box is made of

Nice shining gold from a pirate ship,
Ice, white from the cold South Pole,
Shapes from a spider's web.

Jack Bartram (7)
Nightingale First School, Norwich

Magic Box

(Inspired by 'Magic Box' by Kit Wright)

I will put in the box . . .

The sight of hedgehogs creeping around for insects
                    in the dark, dark night,
The sight of my cat, Milly, catching moths,
The sight of little insects hopping around in the green grass.

I will put in the box . . .

The sound of small green crickets creaking in the garden plants,
The sound of the wind blowing the leaves on the ground,
The sound of birds tweeting in the waving trees.

I will put in the box . . .

The smell of pancakes cooking in the microwave,
The smell of fish and chips in the oven.

Megan Ward (8)
Nightingale First School, Norwich

The Magic Box

(Based on 'Magic Box' by Kit Wright)

I will put in the box . . .

A winter-cold snow,
Snowflakes as pretty as can be, falling to the white snow,
Some sticky yummy chocolate fudge with a cone and some ice cream,
Pretty pink blossom smells like perfume sprayed on you,
Dogs playing with a cute kitten
In a field listening to music,
Fireworks popping, red, yellow and blue,
Laughing in the park with people doing silly things.

My box is made of

Sunsets as big as the sun, glitter glittering on the lid.

Kayla Woods (7)
Nightingale First School, Norwich

Magic Box

(Inspired by 'Magic Box' by Kit Wright)

I will put in the box . . .

The sight of sparkly spiderwebs in the rain,
The sight of my yellow sparkly teddy waiting in bed,
The sight of bees flying in and out of a tree.

I will put in the box . . .

The sound of fabulous noisy nature,
The sound of groovy disco music,
The sound of my brother laughing when I tickle his toes.

I will put in the box . . .

The smell of a cup of yummy cocoa,
The smell of a candle next to the bath,
The smell of pink flowers in the long garden.

I will put in the box . . .

The taste of figs ripening on a tree,
The taste of pancakes cooking for me,
The taste of garlic bread that goes with soup.

Sabina Illing (7)
Nightingale First School, Norwich

The Magic Box

(Based on 'Magic Box' by Kit Wright)

I will put in the box . . .

Sweet melting chocolate melting on my tongue.
My hamster, hairy and cute.
My next-door neighbour's black dog barking.
The cat looking very colourful.
The pizza smelling of spicy pepperoni.

My box is made of ice, lava, gold and fire.

Joshua Wymer (7)
Nightingale First School, Norwich

The Magic Box

(Based on 'Magic Box' by Kit Wright)

I will put in the box . . .

Fluffy, soft fur,
Sparkling, loud fireworks,
Brown, sweet, melted chocolate,
Green, juicy kiwis,
Hot golden-yellow chips,
Black, calm dogs,
Misty, grey bonfires,
Purple, beautiful sunset,
Chewy, sticky pizza,
Cheerful, happy music.

My box is made of
Sparkling, hard glitter,
Shiny magic stars,
Fluffy soft fur.

Jasmine Thompson (7)
Nightingale First School, Norwich

The Magic Box

(Based on 'Magic Box' by Kit Wright)

I will put in the box . . .
The chocolate melting on the tip of my tongue.
The lovely smell of pancakes cooking in the afternoon.
A horse neighing over the hedge.
Candles dancing in the moon.
A cute puppy sitting on my lap.
The chocolate baking in the oven.
The puffy smoke smells a bit like burning fire.
A Dalmatian barking in the garden.

My box is made of fluffy bear fur,
Silver, gold and blue glitter,
Glittery silver stars,
Glittery red lipstick.

India Fincham (7)
Nightingale First School, Norwich

Thunder

I can hear thunder rumbling in the air.
I can see thunder in the air.
Thunder, thunder crashing up high.
What's that noise?
It is thunder booming up high.

I can see thunder in the air.
What can you see in the air?
Now it's 8 o'clock it is time for bed.
I kiss my wonderful teddy goodnight
And we both go to sleep.

Now it's the next day.
It's sunny and bright.
Now I am going out to play with my best friend
To play fun and games in the park.

Matthew Ireland (7)
Oak Green School, Aylesbury

A Roman Poem

Romans are fierce, scary and deadly.
The Romans and Celts are deadly.

Obliteration of killing, sneaking
Roman and Celts.

Massive killing, Romans attacking
and frightening the people away.

Axes are scary, fierce and
deadly and hurt painfully.

Naughty and really prickly
and painful spears.

Spiky and prickly and attacking
spikeballs and deadly,
fiercely enormous machines.

George Guy (9)
Oak Green School, Aylesbury

Boudicca

Boudicca's hair, red as fire.
Queen of the Iceni.
Boudicca, fierce as a tiger,
Fast as a wolf.
Boudicca cruel as a mean wolf,
Horrible as a fox.
Boudicca was very clever for a woman like her,
Strong as a wrestler.
Boudicca had a very expensive funeral,
It was probably the best day of her life.
Boudicca proved that she was as good as a man,
Strong in war.
Boudicca was born before 43AD.
Boudicca grew up with the Celts,
Rose up to fight the Romans.
Boudicca, as brave as a lion.
Boudicca led the Britons against the Romans.

Lauren Howard (9)
Oak Green School, Aylesbury

Firework Night

Listen!
What can you hear?
The thunder crackling up in the sky and booming.
Look!
What can you see?
Up in the sky you can see thunder sparkling.
Listen!
What can you hear?
The sparks shooting up high in the sky.

Lucy Cheriman (7)
Oak Green School, Aylesbury

Fireworks

I can see fireworks in the big blue sky.
I can hear them popping.
But I don't know why.
Which colours are in the dark sky?
There are pink, gold and purple.
I see fireworks in the big sky.
I can hear them popping.
But I don't know why.
Which colours are in the dark blue sky?
This time there are several, pink, purple, black and brown.
I can see fireworks in the big blue sky.
I can hear them popping.
But I don't know why.

Shauntay Francis (7)
Oak Green School, Aylesbury

Boudicca

Boudicca, as cruel as a tiger.
She was as evil as a witch.
Boudicca's hair, as hot as the sun.
Queen of the ice.
Boudicca's eyes, as big as an owl's,
She burnt Verulamium down.
Boudicca's clothes were as soft as a fluffy kitten's
She led the Britons against the Romans.
Boudicca was as clever as a monkey.
Rose up to fight.
Boudicca, as fierce as a lion.
Boudicca died in 61AD

Amy Williams (8)
Oak Green School, Aylesbury

Boudicca

Boudicca, hair as red as fire,
Queen of the Iceni.
Boudicca was as cruel as a wolf,
Had a very expensive funeral.
Boudicca, as clever as a dog,
She proved that women were as strong as men.
Boudicca as angry as a lion,
She died in 61AD.
Boudicca, as strong as a wrestling man.

Amy Turnbull (8)
Oak Green School, Aylesbury

Thunder

I hear thunder
Rumbling all around,
Growling in the sky,
Booming up the sky.
I hear fireworks
Booming at night and in the morning.
It scares me.

Alexander Newman (7)
Oak Green School, Aylesbury

Love

Love is red like roses.
It sounds like birds singing in the trees.
It smells like roses.
It looks like a heart.
It feels as soft as a teddy.
It reminds me of happiness.

Nazmin Akhtar (8)
Oak Green School, Aylesbury

Love

Love is red like roses
It sounds like birds tweeting loudly.
It tastes like sweetness,
It smells like chocolate.
It looks like a red heart,
It feels squishy and juicy.
It reminds me of happiness.

Leighonnie Gardener-Ward (8)
Oak Green School, Aylesbury

Love

Love is red like roses
Love sounds like tweeting birds
Love tastes like chocolate cake
Love smells like cakes cooking
Love looks like flowers dancing
Love feels like a happy heart
Love reminds me of happiness.

Lauren Perry (8)
Oak Green School, Aylesbury

Love

Love is red like roses
It sounds like music.
It tastes like sweetness.
It smells like strawberries,
It looks like red hearts,
It feels soft,
It reminds me of love hearts.

Tahir Taybah (8)
Oak Green School, Aylesbury

Thunder

I can hear thunder rumbling, growling, crashing all around.
I can hear thunder booming in the sky.
I can hear Zeus up high, making lightning.
I can see thunder crashing and it's crashing at night-time.
I can see thunder making the dark in the air.
I can see thunder making the lightning all around.
I think the thunder is going to come.

Aishah Kamran (7)
Oak Green School, Aylesbury

Fireworks

I can hear fireworks popping and banging up in the clear black sky.
The clouds are beautiful and clear.
They make big bangs.
Why do they make colours sometimes but not in the day?
They make big pops and bangs.
When the fireworks are done I go to bed.

Erin McCarthy (7)
Oak Green School, Aylesbury

Thunder

I can hear thunder rumbling in the sky.
Growling all around, making everyone scared in the night.
It lets no one go to sleep.
The next day it was still thundering and raining.
It never stops and the children never stop being scared.

Chantelle McNally (7)
Oak Green School, Aylesbury

Boudicca

Boudicca her hair as red as fire,
Queen of the Iceni.
Boudicca nasty as a snake,
Burnt Verulamium to the ground.
Boudicca fierce as a lion,
Charged through the Romans.
Boudicca tough as a tiger,
Flogged by the Romans.
Boudicca angry as anyone else,
Rose up to fight.
Boudicca as strong as a polar bear
Led the British against the Romans.
Boudicca, clever as a dog,
Burnt Emperor Claudius' temple to the ground.

Boudicca angry as a bear,
Her armies made from farmers.
Boudicca eyes as deep as pools
Poisoned herself and her daughters.
Boudicca fierce as a shark.   •
Died in AD61
Boudicca.

Fathema Begum (9)
Oak Green School, Aylesbury

Fireworks

I can see them spinning in the air.
Making the fantastic colours in the dark blue sky.
I can see the fireworks spinning all around
Making beautiful colours up in the clouds.
I can see the fireworks popping up and down
Making pretty colours that shine and glow.

Fazeela Anwar (8)
Oak Green School, Aylesbury

Boudicca

Boudicca, Boudicca as hot as fire,
Queen of the British Iceni.
Boudicca, Boudicca as sweet as a rose,
Rose up to fight with the Celts.
Boudicca, Boudicca as brave as a lion,
Burnt Verulamium to the ground.
Boudicca, Boudicca as horrid as Henry the Eighth.
Lead the Celts into battle,
Boudicca, Boudicca as clever as an ant
Fought against the Romans.
Boudicca, Boudicca as sharp as barbed wire.

Emily-Rose Baughan (8)
Oak Green School, Aylesbury

Romans

R omans stink like a pigsty.
O ne is fierce and strong as a lion.
M en fight like strong tigers.
A Roman has lots of metal properties.
N ever mess with the rich, rich Romans.
S nails are one of their treats to eat.

Stuart Humphries (8)
Oak Green School, Aylesbury

Happiness

Happiness is like a person playing with you.
Happiness smells like sweetness.
Happiness feels like a newborn baby.
Happiness reminds me of surprises.

Shannon Byrne (8)
Oak Green School, Aylesbury

Boudicca

Boudicca as strong as a row of armoured men,
Queen of the Iceni.
Boudicca as mean as a cobra,
Burnt down Verulamium.
Boudicca as stroppy as a wolf
Flogged by the Romans.
Boudicca as clever as a dog,
Led the Britains against the Romans.
Boudicca as fierce as a rhino,
Often compared to Elizabeth I.
Boudicca, hair as red as flames and fire,
Boudicca was born before AD43.
Boudicca, eyes as blue as waterfalls.
Destroyed three cities.
She hated the Romans and had farmers as her army.
Boudicca was as sly as a fox.
Poisoned herself and her daughters.

Sadia Fazal (9)
Oak Green School, Aylesbury

Boudicca

Boudicca was as rough as a tiger,
Queen of Iceni.
She was grumpy as a man,
Burnt Verulamium to the ground.
She was as muscular as ten polar bears
Flogged by the Romans.
Boudicca wore jewellery that was dear.
Rose up to fight,
She was strong and mighty
Fighting for freedom.
Poisoned herself and her daughters.
Boudicca clever as a dog
Celts believed in gods.
She had farmers for the army.

Islam Udeen (9)
Oak Green School, Aylesbury

Boudicca

Boudicca as sharp as a knife
She died of poison
Boudicca as fierce as a lion
She burnt down Verulamium to the ground
Boudicca killed lots of Romans
She died in AD61
Boudicca as greedy as a pig
She was queen of the Iceni
Boudicca had three little girls
She burnt three countries
Boudicca was greater than a teacher
She was faster than a fox
Boudicca killed thousands of Romans
She had different weapons
Boudicca was cheeky as a monkey.

Jack White (8)
Oak Green School, Aylesbury

Anger And Love

Anger is brown like a burglar
It sounds like a monster
It tastes like bad juice
It smells like mud
It feels like a troll
It reminds me of a lion.

Love is red like roses
It sounds like happiness
It smells like flowers
It tastes like chocolate
It feels like softness
It reminds me of a queen.

Humza Abdul Rehman (8)
Oak Green School, Aylesbury

Boudicca

Boudicca, hair as red as fire.
Boudicca, as tall as a tree.
Boudicca, as sharp as a knife.
Boudicca, as round as a circle.
Boudicca, as red as lava.
Boudicca, fierce as a lion.
Boudicca, as ugly as a rhino.
Boudicca, as mean as Henry VIII.

Tessa Avis (8)
Oak Green School, Aylesbury

Anger

Anger is red like blood,
It sounds like leaves blowing.
It tastes like mud and dirt,
It smells like rotting apples.
It looks like horrible cheese,
It feels like bumpy old rocks.
It reminds me of ugly mud.

Jade Andre (8)
Oak Green School, Aylesbury

Anger

Anger is brown like a monster
It sounds like a burglar
It tastes like mud.
It smells like bad juice
It looks like a giant.
It feels like a troll
It reminds me of the biggest lion.

Afzaal Hussain (8)
Oak Green School, Aylesbury

Boudicca

Boudicca, her hair as red as fire
Queen of Iceni
Boudicca, as evil as a witch
She burnt down the town of Verulamium
Boudicca, her eyes as big as pools
She's as quiet as a tiger
She burnt down the Emperor's temple
She fought for freedom
She had orangey hair as orange as oranges
Boudicca fought to the death
Boudicca, she poisoned herself
Boudicca, as warlike as a warrior
Boudicca poisoned her own daughters
She was as clever as a dog
She had a very hard voice
Boudicca, as tough as a lion
Her hair was waist length
She was as rich as the queen
She had a very rich funeral
She was a strong ruler
She was often compared to Elizabeth I
She proved women were as strong as men
She died in 61AD
She was born in Britain
She was a daughter of a leader
She made a stand against the Romans
She rose up with the Celts to fight
Boudicca, why did you burn down Londonium?

Amber Colley (8)
Oak Green School, Aylesbury

Love

Love is red like blood,
It sounds like music.
It tastes like sweet grapes.
It smells like mango juice,
It looks like your heart.
It feels like crispy ice.
It reminds me of my wedding.

Amreen Ali (8)
Oak Green School, Aylesbury

Love

Love is red like blood
It sounds like birds singing.
It tastes like chocolate
It smells like beautiful flowers.
It looks like a heart
It reminds me of a wedding.

Callum Fallows (8)
Oak Green School, Aylesbury

The Dog

There is a black and white dog that lives on our street,
It comes to our door for something to eat.
He will stand outside and bark, bark, bark.
Sometimes he will wait till it is dark, dark, dark.
And when I've given him a little treat
He will run away back down our street.

Hannah Greig (8)
Our Lady & St Oswald's Catholic Primary School, Oswestry

Brothers

It's not fair, I have more than my fair share,
Why are they like no other?
They take, take, take
And give you bother.
Brothers!

They always think they're funny,
Although you know they're not,
And don't mind sharing your stuff,
But their stuff, they will not.
Brothers!

We always end up fighting,
Especially over bunk beds,
And Mum comes upstairs, shouting
When I've left them both for dead.
Brothers!

My brothers, they spell trouble
Wherever we all go,
Always misbehaving,
And making a big show.
Although they make me angry
I love them both to bits.
I wouldn't be without them.
Well just a little bit.
Brothers.

Michael Hare (7)
Our Lady & St Oswald's Catholic Primary School, Oswestry

Moving

Our house, it took two years to build,
In the end I was fed up instead of thrilled.
But now we've settled in, it's great.
It was definitely worth the wait!

Niamh Maguire (8)
Our Lady & St Oswald's Catholic Primary School, Oswestry

Under The Sea

As the friendly fish swam by
An octopus said bye-bye.
A diver went down deep,
A stingray falls fast asleep.
A jellyfish goes wibble wobble,
A dolphin goes dibble dobble.
The angelfish goes hello,
The starfish goes on tippy-toe.
Lobster goes snip-snap,
Crab goes clippety clap.
The whale is the king of the ocean,
Along comes a shark and causes a commotion.
All of these things you see under the sea,
That's why it's the place for me!

Amelia Gregory (8)
Our Lady & St Oswald's Catholic Primary School, Oswestry

My Dog

I have a dog called Hugo
He is very, very lucky
He is quite a little rascal
And also very mucky.

He is full of life and keeps me busy
Running round and round
And feeling rather dizzy
But it also makes me proud.

At night-time I put him to bed,
All cuddled up in his basket,
He lies down his sleepy head
And dreams of being fed.

Hannah Beaman (8)
Our Lady & St Oswald's Catholic Primary School, Oswestry

My Hamster, Hardeep

My hamster Hardeep, he likes to play,
My hamster Hardeep, he sleeps all day,
At night he likes to run around,
And make a noisy scratching sound.

My hamster Hardeep, he's small and furry,
My hamster Hardeep is in a hurry,
He runs inside his Ferris wheel,
I think his muscles will turn to steel.

My hamster Hardeep, his fur looks like honey,
My hamster Hardeep, he's very funny,
He hides inside his little nest,
He likes to have a lot of rest.

My hamster Hardeep, he lives in a cage,
My hamster Hardeep, he's quite a young age,
I give him nuts and seeds to eat,
He sometimes likes to have a treat.

Alastair Edwards (8)
Our Lady & St Oswald's Catholic Primary School, Oswestry

I Can See The Dolphins

I can see the dolphins jumping in the sea
I can see the dolphins playing happily.
I can see the dolphins splashing about,
I can see the dolphins darting in and out.

I can see the dolphins chasing their tea,
I can see the dolphins hunting with glee.
I can see the dolphins eating their fish,
I can see the dolphins finishing with a swish.

I can see the dolphins swimming merrily,
I can see the dolphins dancing in the sea.
I can see the dolphins cruising through the blue,
I can see the dolphins . . . can you?

Georgia Dale (8)
Our Lady & St Oswald's Catholic Primary School, Oswestry

Charlie

Charlie is my dog,
he's very cute and funny.

When it's raining he wants to play, he looks for the sun to come
out today.
He looks at the rain and looks at me, but soon it's time for me
to have tea.
Charlie follows me when I sit down, but then he gives me
a sort of frown.
He likes my food but I don't feed him any, so he goes and
watches telly.
Charlie likes to chase cats and birds, and when he's called
doesn't hear a word.
So that is Charlie, my best friend, I know on him I can always depend.
Woof, woof, woof.

Emma Jones (7)
Our Lady & St Oswald's Catholic Primary School, Oswestry

Callum Rose's Limericks

There was a boy from Bath
Who was sadly rubbish at math
He had a test
And tried his best
But still faced his teacher's wrath!

There was a boy called Paul
Who thought he was a Gaul
He closed his eyes
And screamed war cries
But walked right into a wall!

There was a girl called Jane
Who went temporarily insane
She was weird all right
But got well over night
And never went mad again!

Callum Rose (10)
Randlay Primary School, Telford

The Scare Game

There's a house on a hill,
Come if you will,
Up to the big front door
Come with me
And you will see
Things you've never seen before.

Rooms a piercing cold,
Walls covered in mould,
Smeared with green goo,
Oh yuck!
What muck!
Is this creepy to you?

Big dark blobs
Look like mobs
Of angry little faces,
Everywhere.
On that chair
In all kinds of places.

A loud scary sound,
Makes your heart pound,
Coming from upstairs,
Let's go up
Have a look
And scare it, unawares.

Come through here
And have a peer,
At our noisy friend,
It's my cat
With *my* rat.
They drive me round the bend!

Laura Pallett (11)
Randlay Primary School, Telford

Mr Davies

Mr Davies is a hyena laughing all night long,
Watching TV if there is anything on.
He goes and spends his money, when it's sunny.
He loves to wear his T-shirt with all his Cub badges on.
He's got golden eagle eyes looking for his prey,
He's a green leaf.
He's a fast Ferrari but he never eats salami.

Adam Young (10)
Rushbury CE Primary School, Church Stretton

The Monster At Elm Street

I know a monster down on Elm Street,
He is a monster you wouldn't like to meet.
Spotty arms and spotty legs and multicoloured feet.
He makes a squishing sound as he waddles down the street.
A little girl got eaten, a little girl called Sue,
And the neighbours say he's going to eat you!

Roisin Goode & Sarah Griffiths (9)
Rushbury CE Primary School, Church Stretton

Guess Who?

You are the colour purple calm and friendly,
You are a hawk fast and clever,
You are an armchair cuddly and soft,
You are a rabbit cute and lovely,
You are a daisy pretty and kind,
You are a bike, fun and soothing.
You are my teddy bear!

Maia Hawthorne (9)
Rushbury CE Primary School, Church Stretton

The Sound Collector

(Based on 'The Sound Collector' by Roger McGough)

A stranger called into school this morning
Dressed all in red and grey,
Put all the sounds into a sack
And carried them away.

The popping of the glue stick
The humming of the light,
The cracking of the paper
The light so bright.

The squeaking of the tables
The ticking of the clock,
The creaking of the door
And the boy had an electric shock.

The zipping of zips
The crackling of the leaves
The screening of the pencil
And the waving of the trees.

The ringing of the bell
The bouncing of the ball
The dripping of the tap
And the bashing on the wall.

Owen Hotchkiss (9)
Rushbury CE Primary School, Church Stretton

Rivers Can . . .

Rivers can flow
Rivers can crash
Rivers can jump
Rivers can bash

Rivers can bump
Rivers can stretch
Rivers can break
Rivers can delta.

Samuel Pratt (9)
Rushbury CE Primary School, Church Stretton

The Sound Collector

(Based on 'The Sound Collector' by Roger McGough)

'A stranger called this morning
Dressed all in black and grey,
Put every sound into a bag
And carried them away'.

The shouting of the children,
The donging of the bell.
The bleating of the sheep
The ear-splitting yell.

The flushing of the toilet
The plopping of the paint,
The creaking of the door
The naughty child's fate.

The moaning of the teachers
In the staffroom,
The munching of the biccies
And they go pretty soon!

James Groves (11)
Rushbury CE Primary School, Church Stretton

James Groves

Rivers Can . . .

Rivers can clash through rocks
and bend into tight spaces,
They can *crash*!
and pop into places.

Rivers can be *loud!*
Stones sinking into the river bed,
water *clashing* and branches snapping.
Falling over the waterfall.
Splash!

Joe Jones (10)
Rushbury CE Primary School, Church Stretton

My Dad

My dad is a recliner
always ready for a rest.

He is a buzzard
swaying from side to side.

My dad is spring,
always bright and cheerful.

He is a quick quad bike,
always wanting to go.

My dad is red, he's
an inspiration.

He is a dog
always ready for a snack.

My dad is a boiler suit,
keeping warm.

He is a magician,
clever and funny.

My dad is the best
Dad, he's so cool!

Kate Woodcock (10)
Rushbury CE Primary School, Church Stretton

Cars Can . . .

Cars can race
Cars can jump
Cars can kill
Cars can break
Cars can be broken
Then *crushed!*

Charlie Lippitt (10)
Rushbury CE Primary School, Church Stretton

The Sound Collector

(Based on 'The Sound Collector' by Roger McGough)

'A stranger called this morning
Dressed all in black and grey,
Put every sound into a bag
And carried them away'.

The donging of the bell,
The bouncing of the ball.
The zipping of the zippers
The creaking of the wall.

The scrunching of the paper,
The clicking of the mouse
And banging of the drawers,
The singing in the school house.

A stranger called this morning
He didn't leave his name,
Left us all in silence
School will never be the same.

Ellie Bytheway (10)
Rushbury CE Primary School, Church Stretton

A Book Holds So Much

A book holds adventure,
Mystery and crime,
Poems or a story,
And brilliant and gory.

It could be a dictionary,
It could be about history
Or geography,
Or arts and crafts.

Books hold too much
For some people -
But not *me!*

Georgina Morris (10)
Rushbury CE Primary School, Church Stretton

Autumn

Misty morning cold and soggy
It's hard to get up, when outside
It's foggy and all covered in dew.

Last night a hurricane blew
The leaves turning yellow
Red and brown, blown down.

Had to go and collect the first blackberries,
Apples, green and sweet.
Farmer harvests golden pumpkins ready to eat.
I'm going to make a scary face
I think autumn's ace!

Tom James Carter (9)
Rushbury CE Primary School, Church Stretton

Autumn Colours

What is red? A poppy is red
Sitting in its barley bed.

What is brown? Conkers are brown
Watch them when they're falling down.

What is gold? A leaf is gold
Sitting in the freezing cold.

What is green? The grass is green
The greenest grass you've ever seen.

What is orange? Why an orange is orange
Just a juicy old orange!

Chrissie Schlank & Amy Caine
Rushbury CE Primary School, Church Stretton

Bonfire Night

The noise and the light
spreading in the night.

The banging and the screaming
lots of eyes beaming.

Fire flames burning
twisting and turning.

Sparks flying
food frying.

Guy Fawkes burns
tosses and turns
with all his might.

Now it's the end of the
burning night.

Rosalyn Price & Rachel Foster (9)
Rushbury CE Primary School, Church Stretton

Autumn Colours

What is red? A poppy is red
Sitting in its barley bed.

What is brown? Conkers are brown
Watch them when they're falling down.

What is gold? A leaf is gold
Sitting in the freezing cold.

What is green? The grass is green
The greenest grass you've ever seen.

What is orange? Why an orange is
Orange just a juicy old orange.

Amy Caine (10)
Rushbury CE Primary School, Church Stretton

Name Poem

S ometimes cheeky,
T elly on every day.
E very day I want to play tennis
P lay all day
H elp my mum
E very day, so small
N ever likes to go to school.

J umping football is great
A mazing animals
M aths are great
E xcellent English
S illy Stephen.

B eds are good to sleep in at night
A mazing books I like to read
R unning, I love doing
N othing can stop me going on holiday
F un stuff is cool
I deas help you work
E very summer camping
L eaping Max does not stop leaping
D rums are nice to listen to.

Stephen James Bertie Barnfield (9)
Rushbury CE Primary School, Church Stretton

My Mum

Mum is a bed, relaxed and sleepy,
She is a warm sunny day, always happy.
Thinking about blue, as we do.
She is like a dress all cuddly, like a bear,
Driving around in her car.
Beep! Beep!

William J Lea (10)
Rushbury CE Primary School, Church Stretton

Name Poem

J am lover (strawberry jam)
A nimals I love
M um is nice
E dam cheese, lovely to eat
S illy sometimes.

D avid's my middle name
A le and steak pie, yummy
V ery good at maths
I nvestigating shark books
D avid and Goliath interest me.

G rumpy sometimes
R umbling stomach, most of the time
I nterested in books
F antastic films I've watched
F ighting mad dogs
I nterested in insects
T omatoes are yuck!
H orsing around sometimes
S trawberries with sugar, yum!

James Griffiths (9)
Rushbury CE Primary School, Church Stretton

My Sister

Jemma is a pink miniskirt,
running like a black panther.
She is always dancing because
she is a disco ball.
She is like a woodpecker.

Her favourite colour is orange.
She is a lovely warm summer day, but after all
I think she really wants to be herself.

Rosie Woodcock (9)
Rushbury CE Primary School, Church Stretton

Fantasy Land

Everything is magical,
Your drawings come to life,
Although I'd be careful some chase you with a knife!

Chocolate world is made of chocolate,
As I think you'd know
All of TV comes to life, Tinky-Winky, Lala and Po!

Fantasy is reality here
Some people eat their socks -
Myths count as fantasy too,
Go to Atlantis, it rocks!

Some people like it, some people don't
Myself I love it, I do!
I have to end this poem now, I need to go to the loo!

Dylan Clark (10)
St Ippolyts CE Primary School, Hitchin

An Alien Came To Earth One Day

An alien came to Earth one day,
My dad said it came from the Milky Way,
So I looked in a Milky Way bar and I didn't find one.

An alien came to Earth one day,
He joined in when my friends came to play,
My friend told me where the Milky Way was,
He said it was in space, the alien said, 'That's where I race.'

An alien came to Earth one day,
The next minute the alien flew away.

Finley Clark (7)
St Ippolyts CE Primary School, Hitchin

Leaves

Leaves look pretty on the trees but lonely on the ground.
In spring they start to grow after the beautiful blossom has been.
By summer they are fully grown and green up on their branches.
When autumn comes the leaves look orange, old and wrinkly,
they sadly leave their home and float gently to the ground.
Winter trees look bare and cold without their leaves
that are their clothes.
Don't worry trees, your leaves will grow back when spring
comes again soon.

Kathryn Brooks (7)
St Ippolyts CE Primary School, Hitchin

The Moon

I lay staring at the moon through my bedroom window,
It was like it was staring back at me,
The moon's face glittered in its light,
The darkness closed upon it,
It was like a shooting star had crashed into it,
But it stayed still and silent,
I felt as if it was following my gaze,
I gently and slowly went to sleep.

Sasha Gill (8)
St Ippolyts CE Primary School, Hitchin

Fairies

When you look around what do you hear?
Do you hear the sound of fairies?
I do.

Fairies sound like leaves making a sound together.
Do you believe in fairies?
Because I do!

Olivia Pastor (7)
St Ippolyts CE Primary School, Hitchin

My Favourite Part Is Me!

I like my toes
I like my hair
I like my nose
But my favourite part is
Me!

I like animals
I like trees
I like you
But I definitely like
Me!

Lucy Lapham (8)
St Ippolyts CE Primary School, Hitchin

Rubert

He's grumpy like a grizzly bear
and he nips you everywhere.

He can be sweet as honey
and his little face it is so funny.

His coat is soft and smooth
you can stroke him while he's having a snooze.

Rubert is my sister's guinea pig.

Fiona Reavey (7)
St Ippolyts CE Primary School, Hitchin

There Was A Woman From Outer Space

There was a woman from outer space
She landed in a volcano and burnt her face
She flew back into space
With her face all over the place
But when she got there she felt a disgrace.

Matthew Andresen (8)
St Ippolyts CE Primary School, Hitchin

How To Make A Sloe Gin

I went to the hedge,
Across the field,
There were the sloes,
What a good yield.

I picked the berries,
Then found the gin,
I pricked each one
And put them in.

PS: For grown-ups only.

Hector MacInnes (8)
St Ippolyts CE Primary School, Hitchin

Our Lovely World

In our lovely world the grass is green, the birds always sing.
In our lovely world the food we eat is nice.
In our lovely world the people we meet are kind.
In our lovely world the animals we see are magnificent.
Thank you for our lovely world and all that is in it.

Rosie Smith-Kalmus (8)
St Ippolyts CE Primary School, Hitchin

I Like Football

I like football
but I don't like rugby
and I like golf
but I don't like French cricket
and I like Olympics
but I don't like American football
and I like basketball
I don't like some sports
but I like most of them.

Finley Powis (7)
St Ippolyts CE Primary School, Hitchin

My Favourite Food

M y favourite food is chocolate
Y um, yum, yum!

F or tea, delicious roast dinner
A nd sticky toffee pudding
V ery sweet and tasty
O n Saturday toasted sandwiches
U sually ham and cheese
R ashers of crispy bacon
I love on crusty bread
T omato soup is runny
E nds up everywhere

F ruit is very healthy
O ften is my snack
O h don't forget the
D rinks, water is just fine.

Rory Shooter (8)
St Ippolyts CE Primary School, Hitchin

Winter's Come

W hite everywhere covering houses.
I ncredible fog as thick as pea soup.
N owhere around you can see grass.
T rees being lit to light up the room.
E mpty decoration boxes being put away.
R aging snow coming from nowhere.
S nowmen being built by creative hands.

C ats are going in from the cold.
O n and off go Christmas lights.
M any people going Christmas shopping.
E veryone catching snow on their tongue.

Daniel Jordan (7)
St Ippolyts CE Primary School, Hitchin

Family And Friends

Mummy is caring
Mummy is sweet
She looks after me
And makes lovely food for us to eat.

Daddy is strong
Daddy is funny
He teaches me football
And calls me his bunny.

Charlotte is special
Charlotte is really kind
She is my twin sister
We play games all the time.

Bea and Lucy are my best friends
And are nice to have around
They make me laugh
We have great fun on the playground.

I am Amber
I am me
I hope you liked my poem
About my friends and family.

Amber Argyle (8)
St Ippolyts CE Primary School, Hitchin

In The Garden

In the garden I like to play
In the garden there are trees
In the garden there are brightly coloured flowers
In the garden there is a swing for me to play on
In the garden there is a tomato plant for us to pick on
In the garden there is a deck for us to eat on.

Zoe Rule (7)
St Ippolyts CE Primary School, Hitchin

Weather

Sunshine is hot,
Snow is cold,
Fog is steamy,
Rain makes mould,
Weather, weather,
All different kinds,
There's so many,
They fill my mind!

Alex Robb (7)
St Ippolyts CE Primary School, Hitchin

Me

Sometimes
I'm gluing
Sometimes
I'm sellotaping
Sometimes
I'm asleep
Sometimes
I'm awake.

Charlotte Voisey (7)
St Ippolyts CE Primary School, Hitchin

My School!

Thank you for my school,
Thank you for the food they cook,
Thank you for the teachers who teach us here and there,
Thank you for the pencils that we write with,
Thank you for everything!

Hannah Skeels (7)
St Ippolyts CE Primary School, Hitchin

My Hamsters

Andy is my hamster,
he is soft and sweet.
I have another hamster called Polar,
he is so big he loves to eat.
They both love broccoli.
I love my hamsters.
Why are they so tame and cuddly?

Ryan Smith (8)
St Ippolyts CE Primary School, Hitchin

Sadness

It is grey like dullness,
It sounds like somebody moaning to themselves,
It tastes like salty tears,
It smells like burning ashes,
It looks like somebody getting buried,
It feels like crying,
It reminds you of somebody dying.

David Curran (8)
St Patrick's Primary School, Downpatrick

Love

It is like a shiny heart,
It sounds like a heart pumping clearly,
It tastes like strawberry ice cream,
It smells like a red rose.
It looks like somebody kissing,
It feels like someone holding your hand,
It reminds me of a kiss from my mum.

Cara Gordon (8)
St Patrick's Primary School, Downpatrick

Sadness

It is blue like a sky
It sounds like a cry
It tastes like salty tears on your face
It smells like a graveyard
It looks like a friend dying in your arms
It feels like a black hole in your heart
It reminds me of my uncle dying.

Cormac McLaughlin (9)
St Patrick's Primary School, Downpatrick

Love

It is red like a heart,
It sounds like music,
It tastes like chocolate,
It smells like a candle,
It looks like ice cream,
It feels like a kiss,
It reminds me of marriage.

Kerry-Ann McLaughlin (9)
St Patrick's Primary School, Downpatrick

Happiness

It is yellow like a banana,
It sounds like laughter,
It tastes like bananas,
It smells like flowers,
It looks like my friend,
It feels warm,
It reminds me of playing with my friends.

James Small (8)
St Patrick's Primary School, Downpatrick

Love

It is red like a heart,
It sounds like someone hugging,
It tastes like strawberry ice cream,
It smells like a rose,
It looks like flowers,
It feels like missing someone,
It reminds me of someone going away
And the love you feel for them.

Aislene O'Connor (8)
St Patrick's Primary School, Downpatrick

Love

It is red like a heart,
It sounds like my mummy's voice,
It tastes like lipstick on my face,
It smells like a rose,
It looks like different coloured hearts,
It feels like a sunset,
It reminds me of beautiful things.

Caitlin Smyth (8)
St Patrick's Primary School, Downpatrick

Anger

It is red like blood
It sounds like someone squealing
It tastes like gas around you
It smells like death and blood
It looks like someone dead
It feels like a sword through your head
It reminds me of death.

Rhianna Palin (8)
St Patrick's Primary School, Downpatrick

Fun

It is red like a ruby,
It sounds like children laughing,
It tastes like lovely sweets at a party,
It smells like fresh hot dogs,
It looks like children playing,
It feels like paint brushes
When you are going to paint,
It reminds me of playing with my dog.

Orlaith Dobbin (8)
St Patrick's Primary School, Downpatrick

Love

It is red like a heart,
It sounds like your heart pumping,
It tastes like strawberry ice cream,
It smells like a rose,
It looks like different coloured hearts,
It feels like the sunset,
It reminds me that someone is
Always there for you.

Carleen Breen (8)
St Patrick's Primary School, Downpatrick

Sadness

It is black like a black hole,
It sounds like a person crying in the night,
It tastes like tears running down your face,
It feels like watching someone getting buried,
It reminds me of going to my neighbour's funeral.

Fintan Milligan (8)
St Patrick's Primary School, Downpatrick

Love

It is red like roses,
It sounds like people laughing,
It tastes like strawberries,
It smells like a baby's smell,
It looks like puppies,
It feels like a furry underblanket,
It reminds me of Caitlin's walking
And Casey's talking.

Terri-Marie Martin (8)
St Patrick's Primary School, Downpatrick

Sadness

It is blue like a sea,
It sounds like a mouse scratching,
It tastes like tears running down your face,
It smells like burning fire,
It looks like someone crying,
It feels like my dog's dying,
It reminds me of my grandad's death.

Maria Mageean (8)
St Patrick's Primary School, Downpatrick

Happiness

It is blue like a sky,
It sounds like the birds,
It tastes like a nice fresh piece of chocolate,
It smells like a sweet flower,
It looks like a warm fire burning,
It reminds me of Mummy tucking me into bed.

Joseph O'Connor (8)
St Patrick's Primary School, Downpatrick

Happiness

It is yellow like sunflowers growing in the garden,
It sounds like laughter from children playing in the garden,
It tastes like a fried egg,
It smells like a frying breakfast,
It looks like my little sister when
I see her at breakfast time.
It feels like a hug at bedtime,
It reminds me of my family all together.

Shannon Murray (8)
St Patrick's Primary School, Downpatrick

Fear

It is black like the night without stars,
It sounds like a friend screaming and moaning,
It tastes like the wind in your mouth when you're running away,
It smells like a horrible dung beetle,
It looks like someone getting killed,
It feels like the cold skin of a person that has died,
It reminds me of someone chasing me.

Ryan Craig (8)
St Patrick's Primary School, Downpatrick

Hunger

It is red like the sunset in Africa,
It sounds like people crying for food to eat,
It tastes like a dry mouth, no water at all,
It smells like emptiness,
It looks like an empty cupboard,
It feels like nothing, like an empty pit,
It reminds me of countries starving with no food.

Tara McCrissican (8)
St Patrick's Primary School, Downpatrick

Sadness

It is blue like loneliness in your tears,
It sounds like a soul shouting for Heaven,
It tastes like drinking water that your soul turns down,
It smells like salty water from the sea in your tears,
It looks like you are out and no heart is left,
It feels like you're choking and no fate is well,
It reminds me of all lonely people and then they're all gone.

Orla Byrne (9)
St Patrick's Primary School, Downpatrick

Darkness

It is black like a dark dungeon,
It sounds like the roar of a deadly dark demon,
It tastes like salty water running down your face,
It smells like smoke making you cough,
It looks like big black caves in a cliff,
It feels like being stopped by a great dark hole,
It reminds me of bats hanging from the ceiling.

Alexander McCormick (8)
St Patrick's Primary School, Downpatrick

Anger

It is red like a ruby,
It smells like thunder on a wet night,
It tastes like people shouting in my ear,
It smells like burning flames,
It looks like death,
It feels like pulling your hair,
It reminds me of a fire.

Rachel Heathwood (8)
St Patrick's Primary School, Downpatrick

Fun

It is yellow like a budding sunflower,
It sounds like people enjoying themselves,
It tastes like lots of sweets,
It smells like good fresh air outside,
It looks like the whole school at break time
Playing outside,
It feels like enjoying time with your friends,
It reminds me of happy days.

Rian Tempany (8)
St Patrick's Primary School, Downpatrick

Sadness

It is blue like a sea of tears,
It sounds like the thundering storm,
It tastes like tears in your mouth,
It smells like a smoky graveyard,
It looks like a dark hole in your life,
It feels like a disgrace and tragedy,
It reminds me of one God who lived and died.

Charlie Power (8)
St Patrick's Primary School, Downpatrick

Sadness

It is clear like a tear falling down,
It sounds like the hissy wind blowing,
It tastes like a terrifying moment,
It smells like an empty room,
It looks like your family leaving the airport,
It feels like a person fading away from you,
It reminds me of when my mum and dad went to Dublin.

Seamus Walsh (8)
St Patrick's Primary School, Downpatrick

Love

It is pink like the symbol of love,
It sounds like an emotional moment,
It tastes like a kiss,
It smells like strawberries,
It looks like feathers,
It feels like a comfy bed,
It reminds me of a hug from my mum.

Declan Trainor (8)
St Patrick's Primary School, Downpatrick

Fun

It is fun like a roller coaster,
It sounds like children laughing,
It tastes like sweets,
It smells like a child's birthday party,
It looks like people being happy,
It feels like dancing,
It reminds me of my birthday.

Olivia McCrissican (8)
St Patrick's Primary School, Downpatrick

Down On The Playground

Down on the playground,
Peaceful but lonely the tyre park awaits,
The gate standing tall like a soldier,
Watching children go by.

Down on the playground,
Balls happily rolling on the swaying grass,
The field dreading every minute of being stamped on.

Down on the playground,
The basketball nets close with tiredness,
Markings yawn with happiness after another day has gone.

Andrew Haynes (11)
St Patrick's RC Primary School, Telford

Down On The Playground

Down on the playground,
The sun sneakily surprises the weary night sky.
As the shadows fall,
Trees rustle in the wind while standing high,
Long and tall,
Suddenly, the children arrive.

Down on the playground,
Tyres groan as children stampede like cattle,
As they actively run,
Basketball posts stand tall in battle,
Hot in the sun,
The day is almost done.

Down on the playground,
Ramps are glad not to see them,
Shivering with pain,
The whistle is the trigger to freedom,
As they will do it again,
The day will die.

Liam Flynn (10)
St Patrick's RC Primary School, Telford

Down On The Playground

Down on the playground,
The basketballs dance in the wind,
As the morning sun rises like a bright star at night.
As the children arrive the basketballs float across the school ground,
The benches awake, alert like soldiers,
As the morning awakes.

Down on the playground,
The skipping ropes slither like snakes,
While being whipped up against the passing tarmac,
The tyre park tired of being jumped on
And laughed at,
As the playtime ends.

Down on the playground,
The rusty old gates swing open then close
Talking to one another by squeaking,
The tarmac is dead with footprints all over,
As the evening comes.

Eilish Ryan (11)
St Patrick's RC Primary School, Telford

Down On The Playground

Down on the playground,
attractive tyres gaze at the morning sun,
now the day is just beginning.
The markers, beautiful as a charm
look at the tyres being bossy like kings at a meeting.
Now the morning is here.

Down on the playground,
it's chaos for the balls, squashed like bread,
waiting to be bumped on their heads.
Excited benches scream like a child on its birthday,
waiting to be sat on,
as playtime arrives.

Down on the playground,
the day is dying.
Playgrounds are damp like a lake.
Fields are sleepy and half awake.
Now the day is ended.

Lauren Gould (10)
St Patrick's RC Primary School, Telford

Down On The Playground

Down on the playground,
The field waits while getting covered in snow,
Tyres patiently wait, contented,
As morning awakes.

Down on the playground,
The football is alerted by incoming children,
Skipping ropes slither like a slimy snake
When playtime came.

Down on the playground,
Where the playground's left deserted,
The shed abandoned, patient but lonely,
When evening came.

Luke Jekiel (10)
St Patrick's RC Primary School, Telford

Down On The Playground

Down on the playground,
The frostbitten tarmac shuddered under the morning breeze,
As the sun woke, shadows formed,
The rusty gate lay, dejected, eyeing the sun, coughing with pain,
Then the children came.

Down on the playground,
The footballs sat like the morning sun as it yawned,
As children stampeded around the playground,
The basketball was the soldier of the playground,
As it chattered to the trees,
Playtime was over.

Down on the playground,
The bell bellowed as the children left,
The night sky, crept up on the land like a joke,
As the trees sat, whispering to each other, silently.
Now the night will rise.

Sam Doody (10)
St Patrick's RC Primary School, Telford

Down On The Playground

Down on the playground,
Battered markings lay, fading in the morning sun,
Watching horrified as the benches silently scream
Like an animal in pain,
Until the children came.

Down on the playground,
Balls sat petrified eyeing the studded boots,
As the dizzy hoops wished they had been warned,
Until the evening dawned.

Down on the playground,
A skipping rope lay whimpering,
As the fear-stricken trees wished they were dead,
While the sun dipped its gleaming head.

Tabitha Heeley (11)
St Patrick's RC Primary School, Telford

Down On The Playground

Down on the playground,
The benches relax,
For the children to come,
Tyres asleep,
Like a peaceful classroom,
Waiting for playtime.

Down on the playground,
Skipping ropes are groaning,
As children turn them,
Pirouetting balls,
As children bounce,
Now the end of playtime.

Down on the playground,
Basketball nets,
Painful but strong,
Bark battered,
Glad and sleepy,
For the next day to come.

Sarah Pearson (10)
St Patrick's RC Primary School, Telford

Down On The Playground

Down on the playground,
Grass is shivering,
Waiting for the children,
Old oak awakes first,
He is the king,
Morning has arrived.

Down on the playground,
The noise is like thunder,
Old benches groan,
Under the weight of the giggling girls.
Basketball nets stand to attention
Like soldiers
This is playtime.

Down on the playground,
Green gates swing shut,
A battered and bruised ball,
Rolls into hiding,
Petrified of tomorrow,
Evening comes full of sorrow.

Lauren Morgan (11)
St Patrick's RC Primary School, Telford

Down On The Playground

Down on the playground
sleepy bark stretches and yawns
as the morning sun rises.
Basketball posts stand to attention
dreading the noise as the children come.
As the morning comes.

Down on the playground
balls jump for joy
like a child opening a present.
Skipping ropes coil like a snake
as the children disappear off the playground.
As playtime ends.

Down on the playground
tyres gasp in relief as the children leave,
like a teacher when the children slide out of the room.
Oily gates yawn as the children depart.
As the evening yawns.

Georgia Cruise (10)
St Patrick's RC Primary School, Telford

Down On The Playground

Down on the playground,
sleepy bark stretches and yawns,
as the morning sun rises.
Basketball posts stand to attention,
awaiting the children's welcome
as the morning awakes.

Down on the playground,
balls jump for joy
like a child opening a birthday present.
Skipping ropes coil like a snake
as the children disappear off the playground
as playtime ends.

Down on the playground,
tyres gasp in relief as the children leave,
like a teacher when the children slide out of the room.
Oily gates yawn as the children depart
as the evening yawns.

Kieran Jones (10)
St Patrick's RC Primary School, Telford

Down On The Playground

Down on the playground
the yawning night has passed.
Trees standing as tall as soldiers,
tyres sweat and sizzle like bacon in a frying pan,
as morning arrives.

Down on the playground
children's shadows appear.
Hopscotch as proud as a lion,
as playtime begins.

Down on the playground
skipping ropes coil like a snake.
Footballs scream in agony,
children charge out of school,
as evening begins.

Joseph Broad (10)
St Patrick's RC Primary School, Telford

Down On The Playground

As the sun rises, the relaxed tyres
Wake in joyful anticipation of seeing the children.
Basketball post stands tall as a soldier
As it yawns the morning hello.
Down on the playground.

As the children run down onto the playground,
Excited balls bounce like a kangaroo.
Scared skipping ropes cry as they hit the floor.
Down on the playground.

As the evening comes,
Happy hoops whizz around like tornadoes,
Hopscotch sleeping like a baby.
Now evening is here,
Down on the playground.

Adassa Palmer (10)
St Patrick's RC Primary School, Telford

Family

I have a dream today,
for everyone to be with their family,
so that the bad are poor with others
and the good are rich in love.

I have a dream today,
that everyone is fair,
without injustice,
everyone glowing with pride.

I have a dream today,
that bad and good are treated differently,
that they're ashamed
and we're beautiful.

I have a dream today,
for children good or bad to be treated the same,
so they could be ashamed of their actions
or *proud!*
I have a dream.

Katy Aylward (9)
Stoke on Tern Primary School, Market Drayton

I Have A Dream Today

I have a dream animals can be happy,
Roam freely knowing they are safe.
Unlike innocent animals being killed viciously.
It's injustice to all.

I have a dream today all people will get food
But not meat, that's unfair to animals.
Let them feel wonderful and free, not scared.
That's injustice to all.

Charis Virgo (9)
Stoke on Tern Primary School, Market Drayton

Poplar

High
as a
lorry
gigantic
as a
skyscraper
vast as
a tower
reaching
up to
the sky
lofty
as a
rocket
leaves
rustling
in the
wind.

Benjamin Viggars (7)
Stoke on Tern Primary School, Market Drayton

Poplar

Tall
as a
tower
lofty
as a
giraffe's
eye
steep
as a
crane
right
up to
the sky
tall as a
rocket
touching
the
sky.

Kallum Brian (8)
Stoke on Tern Primary School, Market Drayton

Poplar

High
as an
elephant
towering
as a
ladder
long
as a
giraffe's neck
reaching
up to
the sky
steep
as a
hill
and
as big
as the
sky.

Jessica Thomson (7)
Stoke on Tern Primary School, Market Drayton

Poplar

Tall
as a
lamp post.
Colossal
as a
steeple.
As high
as a
ladder
reaching
to Heaven.
Tremendous
as a
rocket.
Roots
shooting
under
the
ground.

Molly Marfleet (7)
Stoke on Tern Primary School, Market Drayton

Poplar

Soaring
as a
steeple.
Towering
as a
ladder.
High
as a
giraffe's
neck
reaching
up to
the sky.
Tall
as a
tower
reaching
up to
the
clouds.

Oliver Emmerson (7)
Stoke on Tern Primary School, Market Drayton

Poplar

Tall
as a
tower.
Long
as a
beansprout.
Towering
as a
ladder
reaching
up to
the sky.
High
as a
cloud.
Roots
exploding
out of
the
ground.

Erin Drakard (7)
Stoke on Tern Primary School, Market Drayton

Poplar

Soaring
as a
church
steeple
gigantic
as a
tower
cloud-touching
as a
rocket
reaching
up to
the sky
colossal
as a
giant
silent
leaves
that
rustle
in the
wind.

Rowena Tustin (7)
Stoke on Tern Primary School, Market Drayton

Poplar

High
as a
giraffe's
neck
long
as an
elephant's
trunk
tall
as a
skyscraper
reaching
up to
the sky
huge
as a
rocket
roots
growing
under
ground.

James Whittaker (7)
Stoke on Tern Primary School, Market Drayton

Poplar

Tall
as a
tower
long
as a
giraffe's
neck
high
as a
ladder
reaching
up to
the sky
lofty
as a
lamp post
waving
in the
wind.

Kim Orme (7)
Stoke on Tern Primary School, Market Drayton

Poplar

Huge
as a
flagpole
lofty
as a
giraffe
high
as a
giant's
head
right
in the
clouds
towering
as a
skyscraper
roots
growing
under
ground.

Ben Preece (7)
Stoke on Tern Primary School, Market Drayton

Poplar

Tall
as a
tower
colossal
as a
rocket
cloud-touching
as a
crane
high
as a
skyscraper
leaves
rustling
in the
wind.

Serena Talbot (7)
Stoke on Tern Primary School, Market Drayton

I Have A Dream

I have a dream,
there will be no more weapons for war,
I have a dream,
there will be powerful peace,
I have a dream,
there will be joyful justice,
I have a dream,
for everyone to be *free*.
I have a dream.

Robert Humphris (9)
Stoke on Tern Primary School, Market Drayton

Poplar

Cloud
touching
as a
flagpole.
Long
as a
giraffe's
neck.
Towering
as a
crane
and the
leaves
rippling
like
the sea.

Isabel Randall (7)
Stoke on Tern Primary School, Market Drayton

I Have A Dream

I have a dream
there will be no more big
fishing nets.

I have a dream
the elegant, beautiful dolphins
will be safe again.

I have a dream
the diving dolphins
will be free!

Phoebe Tustin (9)
Stoke on Tern Primary School, Market Drayton

Poplar

Long
as a
ladder.
Huge
as a
skyscraper.
Taller
than a
lamp post,
reaching
up to
the sky.
High as
a tower.
Dark roots
shooting
under the ground.

Emma Moore (7)
Stoke on Tern Primary School, Market Drayton

I Have A Dream

I have a dream for people to stop dying because of different religions,
there has been enough blood on the Earth.

I have a dream for people to be fair to other people,
whatever the colour of their skin.

I have a dream for people to be friends with people from other
countries, and to live in peace.

I have a dream.

Alex Ilchenko (10)
Stoke on Tern Primary School, Market Drayton

I Have A Dream Today

I have a dream today
there will be a cure for all deadly diseases.
All infectious illnesses will cease to exist
so everyone has a lovely life.
I have a dream today
there will be enough food and water for everyone,
severe starvation will be wiped out forever
so everyone can have a lovely life.
I have a dream today
for every child to have an education
and every adult a job,
so everyone can have a lovely life.
I have a dream today
for everyone, freedom, fun and a lovely life.

Ella McDonald (10)
Stoke on Tern Primary School, Market Drayton

I Have A Dream

I have a dream,
I have a dream that we can live together in beautiful harmony,
I have a dream that we can stop the senseless bloodthirsty wars,
I have a dream that we can stop the murderous massacres being
                                                    done to innocent people.

I have a dream today.

Anna Aylward (9)
Stoke on Tern Primary School, Market Drayton

I Have A Dream

I have a dream there will be no more beastly bullying.
I have a dream there will be no more powerful punching.
I have a dream there will be no more cruel name-calling.
I have a dream there will be freedom for all children from bullying.

Mellissa Walford (9)
Stoke on Tern Primary School, Market Drayton

Mugger

Far from Earth and far from the planets,
this little green dot, in space
glowing bright green
hovered over Mugger Planet.
This boy called Mug
or should I say an alien called Mug,
his favourite toy was a jug,
was walking outside when this big cub
grabbed him and took him to Planet Earth.
When he first got there he learnt how to surf.
He loved surfing so much,
he also learnt how to say such.
His best friend was called Kit,
he became very fit
but someone shouted out his name.
He woke up from a sleep,
Mug got very sad that it was a dream,
he went to get some ice cream
and the dream he had was the future.
It really happened!

Meghan Smith (9)
The Norman CE Primary School, Northwold

My Dog Tess

My dog Tess
She can do tricks
Like shake a paw
And she can sit.

My dog Tess
Can run *fast*
And she is good
At football.

Alex Elwell (10)
Westfield Primary School, Wombourne

Night Of Frights

It was dark on that particular night,
When the moonlight was shining bright.

When the ghostly phantoms come out to fright!
They go up the path down the street,
That's where all the phantoms go to meet.

Screaming, screaming
That horrible laugh,
Destroying everyone's sleepy nap.

They go around
Scaring, scaring everyone.

Oh no! I think it's me next
I'd better get ready
I need to be up for the test.

Screaming, screaming, that was so scary,
I had to be brave, I had to be wary,
But the moonlight could save me from phantoms scary.

You'd better be careful
It might be you next!

William Lochhead (9)
Westfield Primary School, Wombourne

Trampoline

I love to jump on my trampoline.
When I jump really high
I see my next-door neighbour.
One day I fell off my trampoline
When my brother came on
And did a cannonball.
I went that high I put my legs down
And stopped but I felt a shock.
I got really dizzy and
I fell off my trampoline!

Richard Flavell (9)
Westfield Primary School, Wombourne

My Best Friend

Charlotte is my best friend.
She is pretty and fashionable.
We became friends in Year 4.
We both look after each other
So we are not lonely or sad.

I bet you that she has plenty of friends
Back in Clewe Road.
In nursery we both used to fight
Over a silly pink dress and I think it's silly.
We both have got a 'Best Friend' application
To know that we are friends.
She has blonde long hair and hazel eyes.

She is sweet and in a way she's a tomboy,
But with me she is sweet.
We both watch the football and cheer for 5V, 5V
And go *boo* for 5D.
We two are the best friends ever!

Isobelle Wells (9)
Westfield Primary School, Wombourne

My Dream

My dream last night was wonderful,
I dreamt about a theme park that was made out of sweets.
The water was a lake of chocolate cream, what a dream!
The rides were made of freshly-baked cake from the oven.
Cake, soft lovely smelling,
Chocolate strawberry and more,
Cake *umm yum*.
The scene was a sight.
The water fountain was Angel Delight!

I was about to lean over when . . .
My mom woke me up, how mean!

Lorna Pountney (9)
Westfield Primary School, Wombourne

Football Mad

Football, football, I'm football mad,
When you lose in football, it's so sad!
Sometimes in football I'm really bad.
I love football,
'Cause I'm football mad!

When I grow up I wanna be as good
As *Ronaldo!*
To me he's the best player in the world.
When I grow up I wanna be like him,
My goal-scoring chart for him
Is filled to the brim!

I love football, it's the best sport in *the world!*
Man U are my team!
I just love football
'Cause I'm football mad!

Callum Elwell (10)
Westfield Primary School, Wombourne

Cats

Cats, cats, cats,
Some of them are fat and tall,
Some are slim and small.
Take care of cats,
Some may wear hats,
But they are all cats.

Cats, cats, cats,
Some of them are big and bold,
Some are light and small.
Cats can be lovely,
But some can be naughty,
But they are all cats.

Chelsea Watkiss (9)
Westfield Primary School, Wombourne

The Birdman

The Birdman, the Birdman,
He dresses in black,
He lives in the Scillies
And lives in a shack.

He carves sculptures
Of all kinds of birds,
He is very friendly,
But he can't hear words.

He has a warm house,
With a blazing fire,
He is seventy years old
And he lives on Bryher.

He has a view of a beach
That beach has lots of timber.
The Birdman is deaf,
That means he cannot hear.

Ben Adams (9)
Westfield Primary School, Wombourne

The Birdman

Seagulls flying everywhere,
Swarming over the cottage,
It's the birdman.

It's a dull and dark day
Over the birdman's cottage.
A black cloak peeking over his shoulder
As he sat in the corner of the room.

Wood shavings everywhere, he loves carving.
With a scoop of sawdust
Brushed into the blazing fire
Every couple of minutes.

Thomas Hussey (9)
Westfield Primary School, Wombourne

My Brother

I'll tell you a story
about Jackanory.
He is my brother,
and we hate each other.

He's not very tall,
he's actually quite thin.
He never puts his rubbish
in the bin.

He has no manners,
he never cleans his teeth.
He doesn't like the smell
of corned beef.

People don't like him
because he never smiles.
His favourite cricket player
is Ashley Giles.

Some people think he's guilty
and they're absolutely right.
He's really such a 'nana,
he isn't very bright.

Stan Small (9)
Westfield Primary School, Wombourne

Charlotte

Charlotte is my best friend,
even though she sometimes
drives me round the bend.

We play together in my street
and when we have races,
she always gets beat.

Charlotte is a busy girl
and sometimes
she is in a whirl.

Samantha Brough (9)
Westfield Primary School, Wombourne

My Friend Sam

My friend Sam
Is as strong as a man!
Although she keeps rabbits
She has strange habits.

She likes cottage pie
With a boiled frog's eye.
She eats rats with bread and butter
And even eats birds straight from the gutter.

She's got wrinkled worm hands
That look like my nan's.
She's got one arm longer than the other
And she looks just like her mother.

It may be her diet and looks
Or just from reading books,
That's why my friend Sam
Is as strong as a man!

Celine Rafferty (9)
Westfield Primary School, Wombourne

The Birdman

The Birdman is really unknown,
Always in black but never, never shown.
He is always, always alone,
And he speaks in a very low tone.

He's deaf and nobody likes him,
His only company is his dog
And has birds surrounding him
Wherever he goes.

The Birdman got his cottage wrecked
By Big Tim.
His models were smashed
Among the terrible fog.

Joshua Evans (9)
Westfield Primary School, Wombourne

My Mad Mondays

Still in bed, my sister!
Shout, scream *scream!*
Rushing, bustling
But still in bed, my sister!

My mum dashes round
The house getting ready,
Like a cheetah on rollerblades!
She is always shouting at me to get up!
But still in bed, my sister!

Me, I just do what my mum says,
I have some time to watch TV
But sometimes I don't get to do that.
But still in bed, my sister!

My dad's gone to work
He leaves at about 6am!
He works for West Midlands *police!*
But he's not a policeman,
He's deputy manager and works on a computer.
My sister is up, out of bed, finally!

James Reynolds (9)
Westfield Primary School, Wombourne

My Pet Lizard

My pet lizard is like a magic wizard
When I look in his cage he is not there
But when I look in the lounge he is on my chair.
My pet lizard hates to be in a gigantic blizzard
He likes to be warm and cosy.
But when he wants some food he is really nosy.
He loves to play in the middle of the day
When he is relaxing he is in his den.
He'll sometimes be caught stealing eggs from a hen.

Daniel Malpass (10)
Westfield Primary School, Wombourne

Lost Nut

Hi, I'm a squirrel
And I'm looking for my nut
Have you seen it anywhere?
I think it's by my foot.

I'm walking through a garden
Looking for my nut
Like a human that's been naughty
My mom's going *tut, tut, tut*.
But I'm looking like a lion
That's looking for its prey,
I just can't seem to find it,
So I'm seeking up this way!

Guess what? I found my nut!
But no, it wasn't by my foot
It is not in a cage
Can't you see it? It's in front of you
Right there on the page!

Sarah Morgan (9)
Westfield Primary School, Wombourne

My School

My school is like any normal school
But when it's playtime,
I know that the teachers can make a poem about it,
Which will go something like this . . .

Standing in the
Playground noise
Watching all the
Girls and boys
Waiting for the
Time to ring that bell
Inside we'll go, out of this . . . *hell!*

(When it comes to lunchtime it starts again.)

Samantha Lees (9)
Westfield Primary School, Wombourne

Meet My Annoying Family

My annoying family.

My family can be annoying
Well . . . let's start with Mum.

Well, my mom
Has short hair
But when she comes out of bed
She's like a roaring bear!
She shouts and shouts
To wake me up but I don't want to
Because I'm all rolled up.

Well, my dad
Goes running for 26 miles
He comes back and looks like a red beetroot
And his hair's like a short black bush
That needs to have a good brush.

My brother
He's sometimes like a girl
He plays with his friends
And gets into trouble.
When he's on the computer
He turns into a bully
And I sometimes think he's funny.

Well me . . .

I'm a normal, relaxed, working girl
Who just wants to play and be at one with the world.

Maisie Duckworth (9)
Westfield Primary School, Wombourne

Meet My Family

When my mom wakes up,
Her hair is like
A field of grass, and
When she's trying to
Wake me up she gets
Grumpy like a raging
Bull, my mad mom

When I go to my nan's
She is watching TV
And she says to me
'I wish it was bedtime.'
She's tired all of the time,
My tired nan.

When my dad picks
Me up the radio is
On and he sings,
But so badly,
My tuneless dad.

My mom cooks my
Tea and she has the
Same as me, spaghetti
She plays with it and
Makes me laugh.

My mom is mad,
My dad is tuneless
And my nan is tired
And my best friend
Is there for me.

Sheenagh Saunders (9)
Westfield Primary School, Wombourne

Jessie Wessy

My dog is called Jessie
And she is rather messy.
Jessie is as gentle as a flower,
But sometimes she's like a bee
Buzzing around me.
She runs round the house
As if she's on fire.
Jessie is as cute as can be
And I can tell you something,
She's one of the best dogs in the world!
Jessie is one
And has bad hair days,
She's as mad as can be
When she counts to ten
And I can tell you something . . .

That's my dog!

Sophie Cartwright (9)
Westfield Primary School, Wombourne

Birthday Time

Do you know it's birthday time?
I do, do you?

I'm going to a birthday party.
It's going to be fantastic.
I can smell it
It's like hamburgers, chips, hot dogs,
So delicious to me.

All my friends are there, like Sally.
She's like a car going so fast, she might crash.
That was fantastic, it was lovely.
Want to come to mine?

Do you know it's birthday time?
I do, do you?

Charlotte Summers (9)
Westfield Primary School, Wombourne

My Best Friend

Her hair is a brunette colour,
She has lovely brown eyes.
She has a sweet little voice
Her hobbies are dancing
And paintballing.
I know that she has one pet,
A cat called Maisie.
I will tell you her favourite
Colour is pink.
Her favourite story is 'Goosebumps'.
She goes to Superclub Plus on Monday
And she is very good at maths.
She is *my* best friend.

Charlotte Lees (9)
Westfield Primary School, Wombourne

The Birdman

The Birdman, the Birdman,
He dresses in black
And he carries a sack
And he lives alone.

But his faithful dog follows
Wherever he goes.
A friend forever,
Right by his toes.

The Birdman, the Birdman
He sails in bad weather, even if he's ill.
He has a cottage on Sason Hill.

Joshua Flanagan (9)
Westfield Primary School, Wombourne

Dinosaurs

Dinosaurs once ruled Earth,
Stomping and stamping everywhere.
Crashing and crunching through the jungle,
They would give you quite a scare.

There are all sorts of dinosaurs,
Velociraptors and lots of big T-rex.
I'd love to have a triceratops,
A big green one called Bex.

All dinosaurs have died out now,
They have been gone for millions of years.
One day a comet struck their world,
Now I am in tears!

Maggie Taylor (9)
Westfield Primary School, Wombourne

Me And My Mate

Me and my mate
Made a promise,
That we would stick together,
But Mom and my dad decided to move
So I have nothing to do.

Now I've settled in
I am quite fond of Wombourne,
And where I live is alright
But my house is better.

Me and my mate stick together
So it's alright.

James Isherwood (9)
Westfield Primary School, Wombourne

Bombs Raining Down

While I'm in my dressing gown,
The bombs are raining down,
It's an air raid, it's an air raid!
The bombs keep tumbling down!

It's 1941 and the bombs are like hailstones!
It's called the Blitz and it's getting calmer.
It seems like death and it is, it is, it really, really is!

I see my parents sobbing and looking for me.
I don't know why they are because I'm dead,
I'm a ghost, a spirit and a ghoul,
I was killed by flying shrapnel,
Otherwise called debris, so sad.

Just 10 I am, just 10!
As I see my death plus my parents
Just a few seconds ago they were killed
Caused by falling rubble,
Our street has become a battlefield.

William Corbett (9)
Westfield Primary School, Wombourne

My Poem

My dog is a Scottie, his name is Mac,
He's short on his legs and his coat is black
And when he's good and sweet all day
Then he's a family dog they say.

But when he's naughty and nibbles the mat
And gobbles his dinner and chases the cat
And doesn't live up to his pedigree
Then he's allowed to belong to me.

Daniella Edwards (9)
Westfield Primary School, Wombourne

My Dogs And Me

My cute dogs
My dogs and me.

We don't like frogs
My dogs and me.

They both like logs
My dogs and me.

We go on little jogs
My dogs and me.

I care about my dogs

Not like frogs!
Not like logs!
Not like jogs!

But sometimes they are both
Dumb, daft dogs.
Leo's like a fast Ferrari
Tally is like a lazy lion.
Oh! if you wanted to know
Leo is a Springer spaniel and
Tally is a St Bernard.

Ashley Smith (9)
Westfield Primary School, Wombourne

Young Writers Information

We hope you have enjoyed reading this book - and that you will continue to enjoy it in the coming years.

If you like reading and writing poetry drop us a line, or give us a call, and we'll send you a free information pack.

Alternatively if you would like to order further copies of this book or any of our other titles, then please give us a call or log onto our website at www.youngwriters.co.uk

Young Writers Information
Remus House
Coltsfoot Drive
Peterborough
PE2 9JX

(01733) 890066